Readers are requested to take great care of the books while in their possession, and to point out any defects that they may notice in them to the Librarian.

This book is issued for a period of twenty-one days and should be returned on or before the latest date stamped below, but an extension of the period of loan may be granted when desired.

DATE OF RETURN	DATE OF RETURN	DATE OF RETURN

William Shakespeare

The Famous History
of the Life of
KING HENRY
the
EIGHTH

Edited by S. Schoenbaum

The Signet Classic Shakespeare
GENERAL EDITOR: SYLVAN BARNET

published by
The New American Library, New York and Toronto
The New English Library Limited, London

First Printing, December, 1967
Library of Congress Catalog Card Number: 67–31106

SIGNET CLASSICS are published *in the United States* by
The New American Library, Inc.,
1301 Avenue of the Americas, New York, New York 10019,
in Canada by The New American Library of Canada Limited,
295 King Street East, Toronto 2, Ontario,
in the United Kingdom by The New English Library Limited,
Barnard's Inn, Holborn, London, E. C. 1, England

PRINTED IN THE UNITED STATES OF AMERICA

Contents

Shakespeare: Prefatory Remarks

Between the record of his baptism in Stratford on 26 April 1564 and the record of his burial in Stratford on 25 April 1616, some forty documents name Shakespeare, and many others name his parents, his children, and his grandchildren. More facts are known about William Shakespeare than about any other playwright of the period except Ben Jonson. The facts should, however, be distinguished from the legends. The latter, inevitably more engaging and better known, tell us that the Stratford boy killed a calf in high style, poached deer and rabbits, and was forced to flee to London, where he held horses outside a playhouse. These traditions are only traditions; they may be true, but no evidence supports them, and it is well to stick to the facts.

Mary Arden, the dramatist's mother, was the daughter of a substantial landowner; about 1557 she married John Shakespeare, who was a glove-maker and trader in various farm commodities. In 1557 John Shakespeare was a member of the Council (the governing body of Stratford), in 1558 a constable of the borough, in 1561 one of the two town chamberlains, in 1565 an alderman (entitling him to the appellation "Mr."), in 1568 high bailiff—the town's highest political office, equivalent to mayor. After 1577, for an unknown reason he drops out of local politics. The birthday of William Shakespeare, the eldest son of this locally prominent man, is unrecorded; but the Stratford parish register records that the infant was baptized on 26 April 1564. (It is quite possible that he was born on 23

April, but this date has probably been assigned by tradition because it is the date on which, fifty-two years later, he died.) The attendance records of the Stratford grammar school of the period are not extant, but it is reasonable to assume that the son of a local official attended the school and received substantial training in Latin. The masters of the school from Shakespeare's seventh to fifteenth years held Oxford degrees; the Elizabethan curriculum excluded mathematics and the natural sciences but taught a good deal of Latin rhetoric, logic, and literature. On 27 November 1582 a marriage license was issued to Shakespeare and Anne Hathaway, eight years his senior. The couple had a child in May, 1583. Perhaps the marriage was necessary, but perhaps the couple had earlier engaged in a formal "troth plight" which would render their children legitimate even if no further ceremony were performed. In 1585 Anne Hathaway bore Shakespeare twins.

That Shakespeare was born is excellent; that he married and had children is pleasant; but that we know nothing about his departure from Stratford to London, or about the beginning of his theatrical career, is lamentable and must be admitted. We would gladly sacrifice details about his children's baptism for details about his earliest days on the stage. Perhaps the poaching episode is true (but it is first reported almost a century after Shakespeare's death), or perhaps he first left Stratford to be a schoolteacher, as another tradition holds; perhaps he was moved by

> Such wind as scatters young men through the world,
> To seek their fortunes further than at home
> Where small experience grows.

In 1592, thanks to the cantankerousness of Robert Greene, a rival playwright and a pamphleteer, we have our first reference, a snarling one, to Shakespeare as an actor and playwright. Greene warns those of his own educated friends who wrote for the theater against an actor who has presumed to turn playwright:

> There is an upstart crow, beautified with our feathers, that with his *tiger's heart wrapped in a player's hide* supposes he is as well able to bombast out a blank verse as the best of you, and being an absolute Johannes-factotum is in his own conceit the only Shake-scene in a country.

The reference to the player, as well as the allusion to Aesop's crow (who strutted in borrowed plumage, as an actor struts in fine words not his own), makes it clear that by this date Shakespeare had both acted and written. That Shakespeare is meant is indicated not only by "Shake-scene" but by the parody of a line from one of Shakespeare's plays, *3 Henry VI:* "O, tiger's heart wrapped in a woman's hide." If Shakespeare in 1592 was prominent enough to be attacked by an envious dramatist, he probably had served an apprenticeship in the theater for at least a few years.

In any case, by 1592 Shakespeare had acted and written, and there are a number of subsequent references to him as an actor: documents indicate that in 1598 he is a "principal comedian," in 1603 a "principal tragedian," in 1608 he is one of the "men players." The profession of actor was not for a gentleman, and it occasionally drew the scorn of university men who resented writing speeches for persons less educated than themselves, but it was respectable enough: players, if prosperous, were in effect members of the bourgeoisie, and there is nothing to suggest that Stratford considered William Shakespeare less than a solid citizen. When, in 1596, the Shakespeares were granted a coat of arms, the grant was made to Shakespeare's father, but probably William Shakespeare (who the next year bought the second-largest house in town) had arranged the matter on his own behalf. In subsequent transactions he is occasionally styled a gentleman.

Although in 1593 and 1594 Shakespeare published two narrative poems dedicated to the Earl of Southampton, *Venus and Adonis* and *The Rape of Lucrece,* and may well have written most or all of his sonnets in the middle nineties, Shakespeare's literary activity seems to have been almost entirely devoted to the theater. (It may be significant that the two narrative poems were written in years when the plague closed the theaters for several months.) In 1594 he was a charter member of the theatrical company called the Chamberlain's Men (which in 1603 changed its name to the King's Men); until he retired to Stratford (about 1611, apparently), he was with this remarkably stable company. From 1599 the company acted primarily at the Globe Theatre, in which Shakespeare held a one-tenth interest. Other Elizabethan dramatists are known to have acted, but no other is known also to have been entitled to a share in the profits of the playhouse.

Shakespeare's first eight published plays did not have his name on them, but this is not remarkable; the most popular play of the sixteenth century, Thomas Kyd's *The Spanish Tragedy,* went through many editions without naming Kyd, and Kyd's authorship is known only because a book on the profession of acting happens to quote (and attribute to Kyd) some lines on the interest of Roman emperors in the drama. What is remarkable is that after 1598 Shakespeare's name commonly appears on printed plays—some of which are not his. Another indication of his popularity comes from Francis Meres, author of *Palladis Tamia: Wit's Treasury* (1598): in this anthology of snippets accompanied by an essay on literature, many playwrights are mentioned, but Shakespeare's name occurs more often than any other, and Shakespeare is the only playwright whose plays are listed.

From his acting, playwriting, and share in a theater, Shakespeare seems to have made considerable money. He put it to work, making substantial investments in Stratford real estate. When he made his will (less than a month before he died), he sought to leave his property intact to his descendants. Of small bequests to relatives and to friends (including three actors, Richard Burbage, John Heminges, and Henry Condell), that to his wife of the second-best bed has provoked the most comment; perhaps it was the bed the couple had slept in, the best being reserved for visitors. In any case, had Shakespeare not excepted it, the bed would have gone (with the rest of his household possessions) to his daughter and her husband. On 25 April 1616 he was buried within the chancel of the church at Stratford. An unattractive monument to his memory, placed on a wall near the grave, says he died on 23 April. Over the grave itself are the lines, perhaps by Shakespeare, that (more than his literary fame) have kept his bones undisturbed in the crowded burial ground where old bones were often dislodged to make way for new:

> Good friend, for Jesus' sake forbear
> To dig the dust enclosèd here.
> Blessed be the man that spares these stones
> And cursed be he that moves my bones.

Thirty-seven plays, as well as some nondramatic poems, are held to constitute the Shakespeare canon. The dates of composition of most of the works are highly uncertain, but there is often evidence of a *terminus a quo* (starting point) and/or a *terminus ad quem* (terminal point) that provides a framework for intelligent guessing. For example, *Richard II* cannot be earlier than 1595, the publication date of some material to which it is indebted; *The Merchant of Venice* cannot be later than 1598, the year Francis Meres mentioned it. Sometimes arguments for a date hang on an alleged topical allusion, such as the lines about the unseasonable weather in *A Midsummer Night's Dream,* II.i.81–117, but such an allusion (if indeed it is an allusion) can be variously interpreted, and in any case there is always the possibility that a topical allusion was inserted during a revision, years after the composition of a play. Dates are often attributed on the basis of style, and although conjectures about style usually rest on other conjectures, sooner or later one must rely on one's literary sense. There is no real proof, for example, that *Othello* is not as early as *Romeo and Juliet,* but one feels *Othello* is later, and because the first record of its performance is 1604, one is glad enough to set its composition at that date and not push it back into Shakespeare's early years.

The following chronology, then, is as much indebted to informed guesswork and sensitivity as it is to fact. The dates, necessarily imprecise, indicate something like a scholarly consensus.

PLAYS

1609–10   *Cymbeline*
1610–11   *The Winter's Tale*
1611   *The Tempest*
1612–13   *Henry VIII*

POEMS

1592   *Venus and Adonis*
1593–94   *The Rape of Lucrece*
1593–1600   *Sonnets*
1600–01   *The Phoenix and Turtle*

Shakespeare's Theater

In Shakespeare's infancy, Elizabethan actors performed wherever they could—in great halls, at court, in the courtyards of inns. The innyards must have made rather unsatisfactory theaters: on some days they were unavailable because carters bringing goods to London used them as depots; when available, they had to be rented from the innkeeper; perhaps most important, London inns were subject to the Common Council of London, which was not well disposed toward theatricals. In 1574 the Common Council required that plays and playing places in London be licensed. It asserted that

> sundry great disorders and inconveniences have been found to ensue to this city by the inordinate haunting of great multitudes of people, specially youth, to plays, interludes, and shows, namely occasion of frays and quarrels, evil practices of incontinency in great inns having chambers and secret places adjoining to their open stages and galleries,

and ordered that innkeepers who wished licenses to hold performances put up a bond and make contributions to the poor.

The requirement that plays and innyard theaters be licensed, along with the other drawbacks of playing at inns, probably drove James Burbage (a carpenter-turned-actor) to rent in 1576 a plot of land northeast of the city walls and to build here—on property outside the jurisdiction of the city—England's first permanent construction designed for plays. He called it simply the Theatre. About all that is known of its construction is that it was wood. It soon had imitators, the most famous being the Globe (1599), built across the Thames (again outside the city's jurisdiction), out of timbers of the Theatre, which had been dismantled when Burbage's lease ran out.

There are three important sources of information about the structure of Elizabethan playhouses—drawings, a contract, and stage directions in plays. Of drawings, only the so-called De Witt drawing (c. 1596) of the Swan—really a friend's copy of De Witt's drawing—is of much significance. It shows a building of three tiers, with a stage jutting from a wall into the yard or center of the building. The tiers are roofed, and part of the stage is covered by a roof that projects from the rear and is supported at its front on two posts, but the groundlings, who paid a penny to stand in front of the stage, were exposed to the sky. (Performances in such a playhouse were held only in the daytime; artificial illumination was not used.) At the rear of the stage are two doors; above the stage is a gallery. The second major source of information, the contract for the Fortune, specifies that although the Globe is to be the model, the Fortune is to be square, eighty feet outside and fifty-five inside. The stage is to be forty-three feet broad, and is to extend into the middle of the yard (i.e., it is twenty-seven and a half feet deep). For patrons willing to pay more than the general admission charged of the groundlings, there were to be three galleries provided with seats. From the third chief source, stage directions, one learns that entrance to the stage was by doors, presumably spaced widely apart at the rear ("Enter one citizen at one door, and another at the other"), and that in addition to the platform stage there was occasionally some sort of curtained booth or alcove allowing for "discovery" scenes, and some sort of playing space "aloft" or "above" to represent (for example) the top of a city's walls or a room above the street. Doubtless each theater had its own peculiarities, but perhaps we can talk about a "typical" Elizabethan theater if we realize that no theater need exactly have fit the description, just as no father is the typical father with 3.7 children. This hypothetical theater is wooden, round or polygonal (in *Henry V* Shakespeare calls it a "wooden *O*"), capable of holding some eight hundred spectators standing in the yard around the projecting elevated stage and some fifteen hundred additional spectators seated in the three roofed galleries. The stage, protected by a "shadow" or "heavens" or roof, is entered by two doors; behind the doors is the "tiring house" (attiring house, i.e., dressing room), and above the doors is some sort of gallery that may sometimes hold spectators but that can be used (for example) as the bedroom from which Romeo—according to a stage direction in one text—"goeth down." Some evidence suggests that a throne can be lowered onto the platform stage, perhaps from the "shadow"; certainly characters can descend from the stage through a trap or traps into the cellar or "hell." Sometimes this space beneath the platform accommodates a sound-effects man or musician (in *Antony and Cleopatra* "music of the hautboys is under the stage") or an actor (in *Hamlet* the "Ghost cries under the stage"). Most characters simply walk on and off, but because there is no curtain in front of the platform, corpses will have to be carried off (Hamlet must lug Polonius' guts into the neighbor room), or will have to fall at the rear, where the curtain on the alcove or booth can be drawn to conceal them.

Such may have been the so-called "public theater." Another kind of theater, called the "private theater" because its much greater admission charge limited its audience to the wealthy or the prodigal, must be briefly mentioned. The private theater was basically a large room, entirely roofed and therefore artificially illuminated, with a stage at one end. In 1576 one such theater was established in Blackfriars, a Dominican priory in London that had been suppressed in 1538 and confiscated by the Crown and thus was not under the city's jurisdiction. All the actors in the Blackfriars theater were boys about eight to thirteen years old (in the public theaters similar boys played female parts; a boy Lady Macbeth played to a man Macbeth). This private theater had a precarious existence, and ceased operations in 1584. In 1596 James Burbage, who had already made theatrical history by building the Theatre, began to construct a second Blackfriars theater. He died in 1597, and for several years this second Blackfriars theater was used by a troupe of boys, but in 1608 two of Burbage's sons and five other actors (including Shakespeare) became joint operators of the theater, using it in the winter when the open-air Globe was unsuitable. Perhaps such a smaller theater, roofed, artificially illuminated, and with a tradition of a courtly audience, exerted an influence on Shakespeare's late plays.

Performances in the private theaters may well have had intermissions during which music was played, but in the public theaters the action was probably uninterrupted, flowing from scene to scene almost without a break. Actors would enter, speak, exit, and others would immediately enter and establish (if necessary) the new locale by a few properties and by words and gestures. Here are some samples of Shakespeare's scene painting:

> This is Illyria, lady.

> Well, this is the Forest of Arden.

> This castle hath a pleasant seat; the air
> Nimbly and sweetly recommends itself
> Unto our gentle senses.

On the other hand, it is a mistake to conceive of the Elizabethan stage as bare. Although Shakespeare's Chorus in *Henry V* calls the stage an "unworthy scaffold" and urges the spectators to "eke out our performance with your mind," there was considerable spectacle. The last act of *Macbeth*, for example, has five stage directions calling for "drum and colors," and another sort of appeal to the eye is indicated by the stage direction " Enter Macduff, with Macbeth's head." Some scenery and properties may have been substantial; doubtless a throne was used, and in one play of the period we encounter this direction: "Hector takes up a great piece of rock and casts at Ajax, who tears up a young tree by the roots and assails Hector." The matter is of some importance, and will be glanced at again in the next section.

The Texts of Shakespeare

Though eighteen of his plays were published during his lifetime, Shakespeare seems never to have supervised their publication. There is nothing unusual here; when a playwright sold a play to a theatrical company he surrendered his ownership of it. Normally a company would not publish the play, because to publish it meant to allow competitors to acquire the piece. Some plays, however, did get published: apparently treacherous actors sometimes pieced together a play for a publisher, sometimes a company in need of money sold a play, and sometimes a company allowed a play to be published that no longer drew audiences. That Shakespeare did not concern himself with publication, then, is scarcely remarkable; of his contemporaries only Ben Jonson carefully supervised the publication of his own plays. In 1623, seven years after Shakespeare's death, John Heminges and Henry Condell (two senior members of Shakespeare's company, who had performed with him for about twenty years) collected his plays—published and unpublished—into a large volume, commonly called the First Folio. (A folio is a volume consisting of sheets that have been folded once, each sheet thus making two leaves, or four pages. The eighteen plays published during Shakespeare's lifetime had been issued one play per volume in small books called quartos. Each sheet in a quarto has been folded twice, making four leaves, or eight pages.) The First Folio contains thirty-six plays; a thirty-seventh, *Pericles,* though not in the Folio is regarded as canonical. Heminges and Condell suggest in an address "To the great variety of readers" that the republished plays are presented in better form than in the quartos: "Before you were abused with diverse stolen and surreptitious copies, maimed and deformed by the frauds and stealths of injurious impostors that exposed them; even those, are now offered to your view cured and perfect of their limbs, and all the rest absolute in their numbers, as he [i.e., Shakespeare] conceived them."

Whoever was assigned to prepare the texts for publication in the First Folio seems to have taken his job seriously and yet not to have performed it with uniform care. The sources of the texts seem to have been, in general, good unpublished copies or the best published copies. The first play in the collection, *The Tempest,* is divided into acts and scenes, has unusually full stage directions and descriptions of spectacle, and concludes with a list of the characters, but the editor was not able (or willing) to present all of the succeeding texts so fully dressed. Later texts occasionally show signs of carelessness: in one scene of *Much Ado About Nothing* the names of actors, instead of characters, appear as speech prefixes, as they had in the quarto, which the Folio reprints; proofreading throughout the Folio is spotty and apparently was done without reference to the printer's copy; the pagination of *Hamlet* jumps from 156 to 257.

A modern editor of Shakespeare must first select his copy; no problem if the play exists only in the Folio, but a considerable problem if the relationship between a quarto and the Folio—or an early quarto and a later one—is unclear. When an editor has chosen what seems to him to be the most authoritative text or texts for his copy, he has not done with making decisions. First of all, he must reckon with Elizabethan spelling. If he is not producing a facsimile, he probably modernizes it, but ought he to preserve the old form of words that apparently were pronounced quite unlike their modern forms—"lanthorn," "alablaster"? If he preserves these forms, is he really preserving Shakespeare's forms or perhaps those of a compositor in the printing house? What is one to do when one finds "lanthorn" and "lantern" in adjacent lines? (The editors of this series in general, but not invariably, assume that words should be spelled in their modern form.) Elizabethan punctuation, too, presents

problems. For example in the First Folio, the only text
for the play, Macbeth rejects his wife's idea that he can
wash the blood from his hand:

> no: this my Hand will rather
> The multitudinous Seas incarnardine,
> Making the Greene one, Red.

Obviously an editor will remove the superfluous capitals,
and he will probably alter the spelling to "incarnadine,"
but will he leave the comma before "red," letting Macbeth speak of the sea as "the green one," or will he (like
most modern editors) remove the comma and thus have
Macbeth say that his hand will make the ocean *uni-
formly* red?

An editor will sometimes have to change more than
spelling or punctuation. Macbeth says to his wife:

> I dare do all that may become a man,
> Who dares no more, is none.

For two centuries editors have agreed that the second
line is unsatisfactory, and have emended "no" to "do":
"Who dares do more is none." But when in the same play
Ross says that fearful persons

> floate vpon a wilde and violent Sea
> Each way, and moue,

need "move" be emended to "none," as it often is, on the
hunch that the compositor misread the manuscript? The
editors of the Signet Classic Shakespeare have restrained
themselves from making abundant emendations. In their
minds they hear Dr. Johnson on the dangers of emend-
ing: "I have adopted the Roman sentiment, that it is more
honorable to save a citizen than to kill an enemy." Some
departures (in addition to spelling, punctuation, and
lineation) from the copy text have of course been made,
but the original readings are listed in a note following
the play, so that the reader can evaluate them for himself.

The editors of the Signet Classic Shakespeare, following tradition, have added line numbers and in many cases act and scene divisions as well as indications of locale at the beginning of scenes. The Folio divided most of the plays into acts and some into scenes. Early eighteenth-century editors increased the divisions. These divisions, which provide a convenient way of referring to passages in the plays, have been retained, but when not in the text chosen as the basis for the Signet Classic text they are enclosed in square brackets [ ] to indicate that they are editorial additions. Similarly, although no play of Shakespeare's published during his lifetime was equipped with indications of locale at the heads of scene divisions, locales have here been added in square brackets for the convenience of the reader, who lacks the information afforded to spectators by costumes, properties, and gestures. The spectator can tell at a glance he is in the throne room, but without an editorial indication the reader may be puzzled for a while. It should be mentioned, incidentally, that there are a few authentic stage directions—perhaps Shakespeare's, perhaps a prompter's—that suggest locales: for example, "Enter Brutus in his orchard," and "They go up into the Senate house." It is hoped that the bracketed additions provide the reader with the sort of help provided in these two authentic directions, but it is equally hoped that the reader will remember that the stage was not loaded with scenery.

No editor during the course of his work can fail to recollect some words Heminges and Condell prefixed to the Folio:

> It had been a thing, we confess, worthy to have been wished, that the author himself had lived to have set forth and overseen his own writings. But since it hath been ordained otherwise, and he by death departed from that right, we pray you do not envy his friends the office of their care and pain to have collected and published them.

Nor can an editor, after he has done his best, forget

Heminges and Condell's final words: "And so we leave you to other of his friends, whom if you need can be your guides. If you need them not, you can lead yourselves, and others. And such readers we wish him."

SYLVAN BARNET
Tufts University

Introduction

Although *Henry VIII* has for over a century given rise
to vigorous, sometimes heated, discussion, it has received
much less interpretative consideration than any other
of Shakespeare's dramatizations of English history; the
two best-known books on the subject, Lily B. Campbell's
Shakespeare's Histories and E. M. W. Tillyard's *Shakespeare's History Plays,* ignore it. Attention has focused
instead on a single great problem unrelated in any direct
fashion to the play's meaning or worth. In the title of his
celebrated essay, first published in 1850, James Spedding
asked, "Who Wrote Shakespeare's *Henry VIII?*", and
scholars have raised the same question ever since.[1] Indeed,
the dean of living Shakespeareans, John Dover Wilson,
has confessed with engaging candor that the chief interest
of the play for him lies in the authorship problem. That
problem is the most vexing to face the editor of *Henry
VIII.* While he may be permitted to regret the dispropor-
tionate attention lavished on a single specialized issue of
scholarship, he must nevertheless recognize that it can
scarcely be disregarded in a responsible Introduction. He
will do well to confront it straightaway.

Spedding argued that *Henry VIII* represents not Shakespeare's unaided work but, rather, a collaborative effort in

[1] The essay, which first appeared in *The Gentleman's Magazine* (August,
1850), is more conveniently accessible in *Transactions of the New
Shakspere Society* (London, 1874), Appendix, pp. 1*-18*. For my discussion of the authorship question in this Introduction I am obliged to
Northwestern University Press for permission to include materials from
my book, *Internal Evidence and Elizabethan Dramatic Authorship* (Evan-
ston, 1966), in which the principal contributions to the controversy are
evaluated.

which he was joined by an inferior writer who composed the greater part and was responsible for the general design, which Spedding found incoherent. This inferior playwright he identified as John Fletcher. Although some earlier scholars had expressed doubts about the homogeneity of *Henry VIII,* no one had previously developed a reasoned case for Fletcherian part-authorship. Spedding's evidence is internal. In the scenes attributed to Shakespeare he finds vigor, reality, impassioned language, and figurative richness; the Fletcher portions are conventional, diffuse, and languid. These stylistic impressions Spedding reinforces with metrical statistics: the scenes assigned to Fletcher are distinguished by a preponderance of feminine endings (an extra unstressed syllable terminating the blank-verse line) normal for Fletcher but excessive for Shakespeare. Spedding's argument was not universally accepted—Swinburne early demurred—but it has proved enormously influential: so influential that the theory of Shakespeare-Fletcher collaboration is even today not infrequently stated as a fact.

The great drawback to stylistic evidence is its subjectivity, which resides to a degree even in the seemingly mechanical metrical tests that Spedding, along with most nineteenth-century scholars, found persuasive. But additional evidence of a more objective nature has been forthcoming. In an important monograph, *The Problem of Henry VIII Reopened* (1949), A. C. Partridge offered linguistic data based on the use of expletive *do* in affirmative statements (favored by Shakespeare), *-th* inflectional endings in the third-person singular present indicative of notional and auxiliary verbs (also favored by Shakespeare), and colloquial clippings of personal pronouns (favored by Fletcher). These linguistic characteristics essentially confirm Spedding's division of the play. Partridge's evidence has been supplemented by Cyrus Hoy in his recent painstaking investigation of the entire Fletcher canon. Hoy finds in the Folio text of *Henry VIII* "two distinct linguistic patterns: one [Fletcher's] marked by the occurrence of *ye* in eleven of the play's sixteen scenes, to a total of 71 times, and a distinct preference for the contraction *'em* to the expanded pronominal form *them*; the second pattern [Shakespeare's] is marked by the absence of *ye,* a preference for *them* to *'em*, and the frequent use of *hath* which, with one exception (I.i) is never found in a scene containing *ye*."[2] (The present edition differs from most modern-spelling texts in retaining contracted forms as they appear in the Folio.)

For the reader's convenience, the customary scene allocation made by those who view the play as a Fletcher-Shakespeare collaboration is summarized in the following table:

Prologue	Fletcher
Act I, sc. i–ii	Shakespeare
sc. iii–iv	Fletcher
Act II, sc. i–ii	Fletcher
sc. iii–iv	Shakespeare
Act III, sc. i	Fletcher
sc. ii (lines 1–203)	Shakespeare
sc. ii (remainder)	Fletcher
Act. IV, sc. i–ii	Fletcher
Act V, sc. i	Shakespeare
sc. ii–v	Fletcher
Epilogue	Fletcher

The dual-authorship hypothesis is, moreover, attractive on other than linguistic or stylistic grounds. Around 1609, Shakespeare's company began performing in the enclosed Blackfriars theater, the lease to which it had recently acquired. Although the open-air Globe remained in use (indeed *Henry VIII* was written for that house), it was gradually supplanted in importance by the new theater, which catered to a select, well-to-do clientele. At about the same time as this crucial change in operations, the premier theatrical company of the age was faced with the problem of the imminent retirement of the playwright

---

2 Cyrus Hoy, "The Shares of Fletcher and His Collaborators in the Beaumont and Fletcher Canon (VII)," *Studies in Bibliography*, XV (1962), 77. Hoy's discussion of the play occupies pp. 76–85; a statistical table of his findings appears on p. 90.

largely responsible for its overwhelming preeminence. How, after all, does one go about replacing Shakespeare? The King's Men could not very well avoid pondering this unenviable question. Their crisis was resolved—successfully by the criterion of box-office receipts—when the company arranged for Fletcher to succeed Shakespeare as their principal dramatist. And what could be a more natural procedure during the transitional phase than that Shakespeare should collaborate with the brilliant young playwright destined to replace him?[3]

Yet it is an hypothesis, not a certainty, that *Henry VIII* is the end product of such a partnership. A distinguished minority of scholars—among them Peter Alexander, Hardin Craig, R. A. Foakes, G. Wilson Knight, and Geoffrey Bullough—have remained unconvinced despite the cumulative weight of stylistic, linguistic, and historical probabilities. They have, furthermore, discerned in the play an organic unity which they regard as more compatible with single than with divided authorship. The concrete evidence for collaboration is, after all, entirely internal and, in the nature of things, inconclusive without external support. Even the welcome linguistic data do not always provide so clearcut a pattern as one might wish, and there is always the danger that scribes or compositors did not consistently follow such minutiae in the manuscripts which they transmitted. It is a fact that Heminges and Condell, the earliest editors of Shakespeare, printed *Henry VIII* in the First Folio without any hint that another writer had a share in the play. Whether they did or did not know the circumstances of composition we cannot definitively say; but, as they were Shakespeare's friends and professional colleagues at the time, the likelihood is that they did. But would they have omitted the work from the Folio even if they understood it to be in large measure another's? Again we cannot positively say. It is also a fact, though, that they failed to include

---

[3] For an excellent discussion of these questions see Gerald Eades Bentley, "Shakespeare and the Blackfriars Theatre," *Shakespeare Survey 1* (Cambridge, England, 1948), pp. 38–50; reprinted in the Signet Classic Shakespeare edition of *The Two Noble Kinsmen,* edited by Clifford Leech (1966).

Sir Thomas More, Pericles, and *The Two Noble Kinsmen:* works of collaborative or doubtful status. It is true, too, that they printed a text of *Macbeth* with the non-Shakespearean Hecate scenes; but these amount only to a small portion of the whole play. The external evidence thus points to single jurisdiction, yet not with such force as to dismay those maintaining the contrary view.

After working closely with the text of *Henry VIII* over a period of some time, and after weighing the arguments of his predecessors, the present editor is personally satisfied that two styles indeed coexist in the play, that Shakespeare and Fletcher are the authors indicated by those styles, and that the traditional distribution of scenes is by and large correct. He also believes, however, that Hoy may be right in detecting Shakespeare's presence in several scenes usually attributed to Fletcher alone (II.ii, III.ii.203–459, and IV.ii), although he would not venture upon any line-by-line allocation.[4] Because the Prologue and Epilogue are such short passages, he doubts that a persuasive case can be made for ascription to either Shakespeare or Fletcher. The view, maintained by the anticollaborationists, that *Henry VIII* possesses a structure of imagery and other features reflecting careful planning does not for this reader carry any great evidential significance as regards authorship. Such interpretative considerations inevitably have a subjective aspect: there are competent critics who do not find in the work the unity claimed for it by other competent critics. And even granting the existence of such unity, it does not necessarily follow that it could have been achieved only by an artist working on his own. There are sufficient instances of dramatists who have pooled their talents to produce integrated works, sometimes attaining (as in the case of Jonson, Chapman, and Marston's *Eastward Ho*) remarkable consistency of texture; just as there are instances of totally incoherent plays composed by one individual. The hypothesis of Shakespeare-Fletcher collaboration on *Henry VIII* is reasonable and better supported by tangible

4 This editor would not, however, join Hoy in also crediting Shakespeare with a share in II.i and IV.i.

evidence than most such hypotheses, and it is probable that the majority of students will continue to support it. At the same time it remains an hypothesis, and there will probably always be some dissenters. For better or for worse, this editor is unstirred by the partisan fervor that the debate has aroused; his firmest conviction is that the problem admits of no ultimate solution.

If the authorship question presents notorious difficulties, the very existence of the play is in some respects awkward. For many, one suspects, it would have been much more satisfying had Shakespeare concluded his playwriting career with *The Tempest,* a drama as magically evocative as the island on which its action takes place. The great themes of forgiveness and reconciliation achieve (so it seems) final form: it is the culmination of the artist's vision. Understandably, readers and audiences have found irresistible the temptation to identify the creator with his creation, and to see in Prospero's abjuration of his magic the dramatist's farewell to the stage:

> I'll break my staff,
> Bury it certain fathoms in the earth,
> And deeper than did ever plummet sound
> I'll drown my book.

> (V.i.54–57)

And then how anticlimactic, after the revels have been declared ended, for their master to return a couple of years later with yet another revel! To complicate matters further, the play in which the timeless artificer now had at least a hand was quite possibly topical in its inspiration, and certainly it was spectacular (in the showy theatrical sense) in its design. If the composition of *Henry VIII* testifies to anything, it is to the committed professionalism of its author: the supreme poet was yet a shareholder in a company of players and not unwilling to emerge from semiretirement in Stratford to provide his London colleagues with a vehicle admirably suited to catching the popular fancy in a moment of national rejoicing.

The occasion for rejoicing was the marriage on St.

Valentine's Day, 1613, of Princess Elizabeth, daughter of James I, to Prince Frederick, the Elector Palatine and champion of the Protestant cause in Germany. During the previous autumn Prince Henry, the heir to the throne, had died, and the nation had been plunged into grief; now the period of mourning was over, and the lavish wedding celebrations—including masques, feasts, and fireworks—signalized the change of mood. A play extolling the reign of England's first Protestant defender of the faith, and doing so in scenes of pomp and pageantry, would be in harmony with the occasion. Act V of *Henry VIII* celebrates the birth of Princess Elizabeth of glorious memory, and (as R. A. Foakes has observed) the identity of name between the young bride and the great Queen did not escape notice at the time. "How much are we, the inhabitants of this whole isle, bound unto our good God, that hath lent us such a princess," declared George Webbe in *The Bride Royal* (1613), "and in her hath renewed and revived the name and nature of our late deceased, ever to be remembered, happy Queen Elizabeth!" Cranmer's speech (V.v.14–62), prophesying the peace and prosperity of Elizabeth's reign and alluding flatteringly to their continuance under James, resembles in phrasing and imagery what was being said in the marriage tracts and sermons.[5]

To suggest, however, that *Henry VIII* was composed specifically for the royal festivities would be to stretch the evidence, for no court performance of the play is mentioned in the Lord Treasurer's accounts for this period, although we know that five other works of Shakespeare were acted before the newlyweds. Possibly *Henry VIII* was the "stage play to be acted in the Great Hall by the King's players" which aroused "much expectation" on February 16, but which was canceled in favor of a masque; but this is mere speculation.

In identifying *Henry VIII* with *All Is True,* a play about

---

[5] The correspondences are described and documented by R. A. Foakes in his Introduction to the new Arden edition of *Henry VIII* (London, 1957), pp. xxxi–xxxii. I owe my reference to *The Bride Royal* to this edition (p. xxx).

the same monarch's reign known only from a single contemporary reference, we are on surer ground: *All Is True* would be an appropriate alternative title for *Henry VIII*, in view of the Prologue emphasis on "our chosen truth" (line 18). A performance of *All Is True* at the Globe Theatre on June 29, 1613, was the occasion of the most sensational occurrence in the history of that playhouse. The event is described in a letter, dated July 2, 1613, written by Sir Henry Wotton to Sir Edmund Bacon:

> The King's players had a new play called *All Is true,* representing some principal pieces of the reign of Henry VIII, which was set forth with many extraordinary circumstances of pomp and majesty, even to the matting of the stage; the Knights of the Order with their Georges and garters, the Guards with their embroidered coats, and the like: sufficient in truth within a while to make greatness very familiar, if not ridiculous. Now, King Henry making a masque at the Cardinal Wolsey's house, and certain chambers being shot off at his entry, some of the paper, or other stuff, wherewith one of them was stopped, did light on the thatch, where being thought at first but an idle smoke, and their eyes more attentive to the show, it kindled inwardly, and ran round like a train, consuming within less than an hour the whole house to the very grounds.
>
> This was the fatal period of that virtuous fabric, wherein yet nothing did perish but wood and straw, and a few forsaken cloaks; only one man had his breeches set on fire, that would perhaps have broiled him, if he had not by the benefit of a provident wit put it out with bottle ale.[6]

Thus did the Globe perish; but (as Stow's *Annals,* 1631 ed., records) "the next spring it was new builded in far fairer manner than before."

We need feel no surprise that the patrician Wotton should express tolerant disapproval at the public staging of the ceremonies and pastimes of the great before the

---

6 *The Life and Letters of Sir Henry Wotton,* edited by L. Pearsall Smith (Oxford, 1907), II, 32–33.

heterogeneous multitude that frequented the Globe. More suggestive is his tacit admission that he has been impressed, if reluctantly, by "the many extraordinary circumstances of pomp and majesty"—impressed at second-hand, for he was not an eyewitness to the performance he recounts. Whatever deeper resonances are implied, *Henry VIII* on the stage was the super-spectacle of its own day. In an Introduction to the play this aspect calls for special emphasis, as it is least likely to come through adequately on the printed page: the life of a spectacle, appealing as it does directly to eye and ear, is in the presentation.

How deliberately does the play dwell on awesome princely occasions! Sometimes these are depicted through the resources of language alone, as in Norfolk's description of the Field of the Cloth of Gold (I.i), or in the account by the two Gentlemen of the trial of "the great Duke of Buckingham" by his peers at Westminster Hall (II.i), or in the third Gentleman's narration of the solemn ritual at the coronation of Queen Anne in Westminster Abbey (IV.i). But, where possible, stirring events are dramatized. We attend Wolsey's splendid banquet and masque; we witness Katherine's vision of dancing, white-robed spirits; we become bystanders when Anne returns with her retinue from the Abbey. The *dramatis personae* for *Henry VIII* is the largest for any play in the canon, and for such episodes as the procession in Act IV the company must have pressed into service all of its available personnel. The extended stage directions, authorial in origin, show an unusual regard for the proper disposition of the players in the big scenes. For Katherine's trial

> *The King takes place under the cloth of state; the two Cardinals sit under him as judges. The Queen takes place some distance from the King. The Bishops place themselves on each side the court in manner of a consistory; below them, the Scribes. The Lords sit next the Bishops. The rest of the Attendants stand in convenient order about the stage.*
>
> (II.iv.s.d.)

The gorgeous costumes of princes, prelates, and function-
aries contributed to the visual magnificence of these
scenes, as did the impressive assortment of stage properties, including the purse with the Great Seal, the silver
cross, silver mace, and silver pillars, the gold scepter and
collars of S's, the gilt copper crown, gold crown, and gold
coronals and demicoronals.

These visual effects were complemented and enhanced
by sound, which is called for throughout. Patience, Queen
Katherine's woman, sings of the miraculous powers of
"sweet music" as she accompanies herself on the lute.
Such soothing moments, however, are rare: on other occasions we hear the blended voices of the choristers, the
sound of oboes and cornets, the sterner notes of drum and
trumpet, the roar of the cannon. *Henry VIII* is an un-
abashedly noisy play, guaranteed to keep even the drows-
iest spectator awake. "Some come to take their ease,"
the Epilogue declares,

> And sleep an act or two; but those, we fear,
> W'have frighted with our trumpets. . .
>
> (lines 3–4)

Of the several companies performing in London at the
time, only the King's Men had the resources to do justice
to such a play. The destruction of the theater during what
was possibly the premier performance is not without a certain ironic fitness: it was the spectacular effect to end
(literally) all spectacular effects.

In the most notable modern revival of *Henry VIII,*
produced by Tyrone Guthrie at Stratford-on-Avon in
1949–50, the director fully exploited the opportunities for
processional pageantry, display, and crowd movement.
For such exploitation the earliest theatrical precedents
and the text itself (as we have noted) afford ample warrant. These features of the play have contributed to the
dissatisfaction with it expressed by some commentators:
spectacle, being nonverbal, has always prompted con-
descension or worse on the part of critics whose orienta-

tion is literary or philosophical rather than theatrical. "The Spectacle," Aristotle observed in the *Poetics,* "has, indeed, an emotional attraction of its own, but, of all the parts, it is the least artistic, and connected least with the art of poetry." Even granting the validity of the judgment, the propriety of applying to another genre the criteria Aristotle formulated for tragedy may be doubtful. For although *Henry VIII* dramatizes several individual tragedies —Buckingham's, Katherine's, Wolsey's—it is not itself a tragedy but a history play concerned more with the public conduct of its personages than with their buried lives; its intention is to stage, in Wotton's words, "some principal pieces of the reign of Henry VIII."

Clowning and buffoonery of the kind found in Samuel Rowley's *When You See Me You Know Me* (1605), which deals with the same reign, are rejected in favor of an appropriate seriousness and dignity of tone, although the rejection is fortunately not so sweeping as to exclude humor altogether: witness the bawdry of the old Lady (II.iii) and the low comedy of the Porter and his man (V.iv). The repeated stress in the Prologue is on the historical genuineness of the play's people and events, their reality:

> Think ye see
> The very persons of our noble story
> As they were living.
>
> (lines 25–27)

The pursuit of historical verisimilitude (whether achieved or not) obviously limits the playwright's freedom to select, shape, and explore events. It cannot be claimed that the genre represents the highest form to which dramatic art may aspire, but there can be no denying its perennial appeal to theatergoers; of plays produced in recent years, Peter Shaffer's spectacular dramatization of Pizarro's conquest of Peru, *The Royal Hunt of the Sun,* perhaps most closely approximates the type. *Henry VIII* is best understood—and appreciated—on its own terms.

Those terms are not, however, confined to spectacle. Again the Prologue helpfully gives a clue to purpose. The audience is instructed in how to respond to the calamities befalling the eminent personages whose careers will unfold before it:

> Think you see them great,
> And followed with the general throng and sweat
> Of thousand friends. Then, in a moment, see
> How soon this mightiness meets misery;
> And if you can be merry then, I'll say
> A man may weep upon his wedding day.
>
> (lines 27–32)

These lines suggest the evanescence of worldly glory. Fortune, the blind goddess, raises her favorites high upon her wheel, then capriciously flings them to earth. It is an old theme; in the permutations of Fortune's wheel medieval writers discerned the quintessential tragic pattern. According to Chaucer's Monk, in *The Canterbury Tales,*

> Tragedie is to seyn a certeyn storie,
> As olde bookes maken us memorie,
> Of hym that stood in greet prosperitee,
> And is yfallen out of heigh degree
> Into myserie, and endeth wrecchedly.
>
> (Prologue, Monk's Tale, 1973–77)

Henry VIII presents, in the context of Renaissance court life, a trio of such falls from high degree.

The victims, so different in their characters and lives, share not only a common fortune but also, at the last, a common pathos, which they fully savor. Buckingham's stoic forbearance in the face of death gives place in his final words to a self-pitying note, however sober and controlled:

> All good people,
> Pray for me! I must now forsake ye; the last hour
> Of my long weary life is come upon me.

> Farewell!
> And when you would say something that is sad,
> Speak how I fell. I have done, and God forgive me.
>
> (II.i.131–36)

No sooner has he departed the scene than the two Gentlemen, having lamented his passing, discuss the impending
fall of Katherine in almost identical terms (" 'Tis woeful"). The discarded Queen, "sick to death," is granted
a dream of eternal happiness to come. In a last assertion
of regal greatness, she dismisses an unintentionally negligent messenger, then prepares for the end. "I must to
bed," she cries to Patience;

> Call in more women. When I am dead, good wench,
> Let me be used with honor. Strew me over
> With maiden flowers, that all the world may know
> I was a chaste wife to my grave. Embalm me,
> Then lay me forth. Although unqueened, yet like
> A queen and daughter to a king, inter me.
> I can no more.
>
> (IV.ii.167–73)

It is perhaps the play's most affecting moment.

The most stunning of the three downfalls, however, is
that of Wolsey. For a suitable epitaph we may turn to a
contemporary of Shakespeare who suffered a fate analogous to that of the Cardinal. "The rising unto place is
laborious," Francis Bacon wrote in his essay "Of Great
Place,"

> and by pains men come to greater pains; and it is
> sometimes base; and by indignities men come to dignities.
> The standing is slippery, and the regress is either a down-
> fall or at least an eclipse, which is a melancholy thing.

Although the Cardinal is not the play's protagonist, his
cold presence dominates the first three acts. Somehow he
must be humanized in defeat, and in the space of a hun-

dred lines the arrogant prince of the church is humbled
and reconciled to his new condition. Like Katherine and
Buckingham, he prays for his King. He also shows solici-
tude for the future of his servant Cromwell, and for the
first time we do not suspect a selfish motive lurking behind the apparent altruism. Wolsey weeps—the scene is
frankly sentimental—and repents (a trifle smugly) his
worldliness:

> O Cromwell, Cromwell,
> Had I but served my God with half the zeal
> I served my King, he would not in mine age
> Have left me naked to mine enemies.
>
> (III.ii.454–57)

There is only slight foreshadowing (in II.ii) of Wolsey's
fall, and the transformation itself, read in the study, seems
somewhat abrupt; but in a spectacular drama of compar-
atively external nature, subtle nuances of character portrayal are hardly required. The scene has worked superbly
well on the stage, as is attested by the fact that the rôle
of Wolsey has attracted a number of great actors, among
them Kemble, Macready, and Kean.

If the three successive falls from greatness are well
contrived to move an audience to generous sympathy, they
do not engage the deeper tragic emotions, nor were they
intended to do so, as the larger pattern of the play makes
clear. Scenes of calamity alternate throughout with happier occasions. The splendid festivities in York House
(I.iv), for example, follow hard upon the Surveyor's
devastating testimony against Buckingham; the gaiety of
the masque is in turn succeeded by the somber episode of
the Duke's entry after his arraignment. At the same time
that Katherine's misfortunes press in upon her, we watch
Ann Bullen's star rise. And so on. Such juxtapositions are
not unusual in Elizabethan plays, nor, for that matter, in
dramatic art generally, but in this case the total effect is
of a complex tonal and thematic orchestration.

In the concluding movement of *Henry VIII,* in which
the grand design stands fully revealed, the joyous strain

triumphs. The fourth—and last—of the threatened falls does not come to pass. Cranmer, who never aspired to greatness, is tested in the crucible of courtly intrigue. Like his predecessors, he is the object of plots, but he undergoes special humiliations: the Archbishop of Canterbury is made to cool his heels outside the council chamber door with grooms and lackeys. Yet he emerges unscathed, and no heads roll as a result. Instead there is forgiveness and reconciliation, in which Cranmer, his accusers, and the King all participate. The Archbishop can then go on to officiate at the christening of Princess Elizabeth and to utter the speeches of prophetic rapture in the final scene. Machinations have ceased. Some private individuals, most notably Katherine, have in the course of the drama suffered unjust deprivations, but the commonwealth has prospered. A newborn infant symbolizes happier days to come.

Henry VIII is unique among Shakespeare's histories in not depicting an England at war or under the threat of war. Thematically the play has closer links with the immediately preceding romances than with the two historical tetralogies of a previous decade. We are not so far removed after all from the world of *The Tempest,* in which sinister plots are thwarted, enemies are reconciled, and hopeful auguries attend a younger generation. In the character of Henry, who presides over the action by exercising the quasi-magical prerogatives of kingship, we have a figure in some ways analogous to Prospero.[7]

The destinies of all the principal personages lie in Henry's hands. A Buckingham or a Wolsey or a Katherine may absorb attention for a time, but they all pass from the stage, not to return; Henry abides, and his presence gives a measure of narrative unity to heterogeneous events. Yet his actual rôle is limited—he speaks fewer than 450 lines—and the King makes no appearance whatever in

---

[7] The relationship of *Henry VIII* to Shakespeare's last plays is explored with penetrating subtlety (occasionally oversubtlety) by Foakes in the new Arden edition, Introduction, pp. xxxvii–lxii. Foakes also deals perceptively with the themes and structure of the play.

Act IV. No very searching portrayal of him is attempted in the play that bears his name. For a modern audience he must present difficulties: the figure cut by Shakespeare's Henry differs so strikingly from the popular image derived from more recent histories or from films and stage plays. In the Jacobean Henry we do not see the insatiable thirster after sovereignty or the profligate who squandered his parsimonious father's treasure in pursuit of the sport of kings. Nor do we see the gourmand and sensualist, the devourer of drumsticks and wives. Great events associated with Henry's reign lie outside the scope of the action: the Reformation and the dissolution of the monasteries, the martyrdom of Sir Thomas More, the execution of Anne Boleyn three brief years after the christening celebrated in the play.

The Henry of *The Famous History* wears the mantle of royalty securely. At first, it is true, his exalted position shields him from knowledge of the intrigues in his own court; he has never heard of Wolsey's oppressive tax scheme for which (as a matter of historical fact) Henry himself was responsible. But as the action unfolds, his awareness, and hence his authority, increase. Once he knows about Wolsey's perfidy, he rejects the Cardinal decisively. In the Cranmer episode, Henry controls all the strings, but the manipulation serves national interests rather than any need for self-aggrandizement. Thus he would appear to approximate closely enough the popular patriot-monarch lauded by Holinshed and the other Tudor apologists.

But what are we to make of the divorce? Much attention is given in the play to the King's conscientious scruple —after over twenty years of wedlock!—about the propriety of his marriage to the widow of his own brother. On this issue of a wounded conscience Henry meditates privately, expatiates at length in public, and seeks counsel from the most learned scholars in Christendom. Yet before any divorce is bruited, we see him evidently attracted to the woman who will become his next wife. And before Katherine's trial—the results of which are a foregone conclusion—there is Suffolk's cynically revealing aside:

> *Chamberlain.* It seems the marriage with his brother's
> wife
>   Has crept too near his conscience.
> *Suffolk.* [*Aside*]   No, his conscience
>   Has crept too near another lady.

                                             (II.ii.15–17)

Historically Henry's reasons for a divorce were several, but the overriding consideration was his need to continue the succession with a male heir, which Katherine had failed to produce and was no longer capable of producing. This motive is not glossed over in the play—indeed Henry dwells on it at length (II.iv.186–99)—but the force of the point is blunted by the weight given to the King's scruple.

  The problem is further complicated by the fact that the dramatists provide Henry with no self-revelatory soliloquies and by the related fact that his public pronouncements cannot always be taken at face value. In open court he declares:

> Prove but our marriage lawful, by my life
> And kingly dignity, we are contented
> To wear our mortal state to come with her,
> Katherine our queen, before the primest creature
> That's paragoned o' th' world.

                                             (II.iv.226–30)

This does not sound insincere, but hard upon Henry's tribute to his sweet bedfellow comes an aside (235–40) in which he expresses impatience with the "dilatory sloth and tricks of Rome" that hinder the divorce; and in the next scene we have Katherine's complaint that he has long ceased to love her. It is as though the dramatists, having set out to extol Henry and, through him, England, were nevertheless unable—or unwilling—entirely to suppress undercurrents of motive and policy inconsistent with so simplified a view of him. The effect is of a disturbing ambiguity of character.

  It is not the play's only ambiguity. Buckingham presents

a similar problem, although to a lesser degree. Is he in fact a traitor or is he a wholly innocent sacrifice to Wolsey's malice? Our first inclination is to regard the Duke simply as the victim of a frame-up, and certainly much weight is given to his wrongs. In the sympathetically conceived Katherine he has a stalwart defender. The chief witness against him bears, we know, a personal grudge, and Buckingham protests his innocence in moving terms as he goes to the block. Yet the King's anger in I.ii has a righteous accent, and if he is responsible, however unwittingly, for a judicial murder, he is not afterwards disturbed by it. The Surveyor's testimony is never rebutted. Buckingham himself admits that, "upon the premises," he has been justly tried by his peers, and the Second Gentleman's last remark about him has a proviso: "If the Duke be guiltless . . ." After Buckingham's last exit, fairly early in the play, little is made of the matter apart from an inconclusive exchange between Surrey and Wolsey in III.ii. The "woefulness" of Buckingham's fall we do not question, but his degree of actual guilt—if any—remains in doubt. A faint unease persists in the reader's mind.[8]

Such puzzlements, which have prompted reservations about the play on the part of some critics, loom larger in the study than on the stage. In the theater attention focuses first on the splendor and fanfare of the grand processional entries and the ceremonies of public life. The contrastingly intimate scenes, in which a young maid of honor is shown royal favor while her defeated elders confront isolation and imminent death, appeal more directly to the emotions, if on no very profound level. Then there are the great set speeches: we are stirred by the eloquence—impassioned or elegiac—of Buckingham's apologia, Katherine's defense of the sanctity of her marriage, and Wolsey's long farewell to all his greatness. And finally, along with the multitude on the stage and in the audience, we are swept up in the visionary ecstasy of the ritualistic episode of the christening. *Henry VIII* is Shake-

[8] Compare the treatment of this question in the source, below, pp. 177–81.

speare's festive history. It is appropriate that the play was chosen for performance at the Old Vic in London in 1953 to celebrate the coronation of Queen Elizabeth II.

S. Schoenbaum
Northwestern University

KING HENRY THE EIGHTH

King Henry the Eighth
Cardinal Wolsey
Cardinal Campeius
Capucius, ambassador from the Emperor Charles V
Cranmer, Archbishop of Canterbury
Duke of Norfolk
Duke of Buckingham
Duke of Suffolk
Earl of Surrey
Lord Chamberlain
Lord Chancellor
Gardiner, Bishop of Winchester
Bishop of Lincoln
Lord Abergavenny
Lord Sands
Sir Henry Guildford
Sir Thomas Lovell
Sir Anthony Denny
Sir Nicholas Vaux
Secretaries to Wolsey
Cromwell, servant to Wolsey
Griffith, gentleman usher to Queen Katherine
Three Gentlemen
Doctor Butts, physician to the King
Garter King-at-Arms
Surveyor to the Duke of Buckingham
Brandon, and a Sergeant-at-Arms
Door-keeper of the Council-chamber
Page to Gardiner. A Crier
Porter, and his Man

Queen Katherine, wife to King Henry, afterward divorced
Anne Bullen, her Maid of Honor, afterward Queen
An old Lady, friend to Anne Bullen
Patience, woman to Queen Katherine

Several Lords and Ladies in the Dumb Shows; Women
    attending upon the Queen; Scribes, Officers, Guards, and
    other Attendants; Spirits

Scene: London; Westminster; Kimbolton]

The Famous History
of the Life of
KING HENRY THE
EIGHTH

THE PROLOGUE

I come no more to make you laugh.° 1 Things now
That bear a weighty and a serious brow,
Sad, high, and working,° full of state° and woe,
Such noble scenes as draw the eye to flow,
We now present. Those that can pity, here   5
May, if they think it well, let fall a tear:
The subject will deserve it. Such as give
Their money out of hope they may believe
May here find truth° too. Those that come to see
Only a show or two, and so agree   10
The play may pass, if they be still and willing,
I'll undertake may see away their shilling°

1 The degree sign (°) indicates a footnote, which is keyed to the
text by line number. Text references are printed in **boldface** type;
the annotation follows in roman type.
Prologue   1 **no more to make you laugh** (the previous play was
presumably a comedy)   3 **Sad, high, and working** serious, elevated,
and moving   3 **state** dignity   9 **truth** (possibly alluding to the play's
alternative title, *All Is True*)   12 **shilling** (the admission price for
an expensive seat near the stage)

Richly in two short hours.° Only they
That come to hear a merry bawdy play,
15 A noise of targets,° or to see a fellow
In a long motley coat guarded with yellow,°
Will be deceived;° for, gentle hearers, know,
To rank our chosen truth with such a show
As fool and fight is, beside forfeiting
20 Our own brains and the opinion that we bring
To make that only true we now intend,°
Will leave us never an understanding friend.°
Therefore, for goodness' sake, and as you are known
The first and happiest hearers of the town,°
25 Be sad, as we would make ye. Think ye see
The very persons of our noble story
As° they were living. Think you see them great,
And followed with the general throng and sweat
Of thousand friends. Then, in a moment, see
30 How soon this mightiness meets misery;
And if you can be merry then, I'll say
A man may weep upon his wedding day.

---

13 **two short hours** (a conventional reference to performance duration; not to be taken literally)   15 **targets** shields   16 **In a long . . . yellow** i.e., in the parti-colored costume of the professional fool, trimmed ("guarded") in yellow   17 **deceived** disappointed   19–21 **beside forfeiting . . . intend** besides abandoning any claims to intelligence and our reputation for aiming to present only the truth   22 **an understanding friend** (perhaps alluding to the groundlings—spectators standing under the stage—who were sometimes ironically praised for their "understanding")   24 **first and happiest hearers of the town** i.e., the best and most favorably disposed audience in London   27 **As** as if

ACT I

Scene I. [*London. An antechamber in the palace.*]

Enter the Duke of Norfolk at one door; at the other the Duke of Buckingham and the Lord Abergavenny.

Buckingham. Good morrow, and well met. How have
    ye done
Since last we saw° in France?

Norfolk.   I thank your Grace,
Healthful, and ever since a fresh° admirer
Of what I saw there.

Buckingham.   An untimely ague°
Stayed me a prisoner in my chamber when   *5*
Those suns of glory,° those two lights of men,
Met in the vale of Andren.

Norfolk.   'Twixt Guynes and Arde.°
I was then present; saw them salute on horseback;
Beheld them when they lighted,° how they clung
In their embracement, as° they grew together;   *10*
Which had they, what four throned ones could
    have weighed°
Such a compounded one?

I.i.2 **saw** saw one another   3 **fresh** ready, eager   4 **ague** fever   6 **suns of glory** i.e., Henry VIII and Francis I (with perhaps a quibble on "suns" = sons)   7 **Guynes and Arde** (towns in Picardy lying on either side of the valley of Andren; Guynes was in English, Arde in French hands)   9 **lighted** alighted   10 **as** as if   11 **weighed** audience in London   27 **As** as if

Buckingham.   All the whole time
I was my chamber's prisoner.°

Norfolk.   Then you lost
The view of earthly glory. Men might say,
15 Till this time pomp was single,° but now married
To one above itself.° Each following day
Became the next day's master,° till the last
Made former wonders its. Today the French,
All clinquant,° all in gold, like heathen gods,
20 Shone down the English; and tomorrow they
Made Britain India:° every man that stood
Showed like a mine. Their dwarfish pages were
As cherubins, all gilt. The madams° too,
Not used to toil, did almost sweat to bear
25 The pride° upon them, that their very labor
Was to them as a painting.° Now this masque°
Was cried° incomparable, and th' ensuing night
Made it a fool and beggar. The two kings,
Equal in luster, were now best, now worst,
30 As presence° did present them: him in eye
Still him in praise;° and being present both,
'Twas said they saw but one, and no discerner
Durst wag his tongue in censure.° When these suns
(For so they phrase° 'em) by their heralds chal-
lenged
35 The noble spirits to arms, they did perform
Beyond thought's compass, that former fabulous
story,°

12-13 **All the whole . . . prisoner** (historically, he was in fact
present, whereas Norfolk was in England at the time)   15 **single**
i.e., relatively modest   15-16 **married/To one above itself** united
to constitute a greater pomp   16-17 **Each following . . . master**
each day taught something to the next, which superseded it ("master"
= teacher)   19 **clinquant** glittering   21 **India** (probably not India
but the New World, whose gold mines yielded fabulous wealth)
23 **madams** ladies   25 **pride** finery   25-26 **their very labor . . .
painting** their very exertion made them flushed, as if rouged   26
masque courtly spectacle   27 **cried** declared   30 **presence** being in
public   30-31 **him in eye . . . praise** the one seen was always the
one praised   32-33 **no discerner . . . censure** i.e., no beholder dared
choose one above the other   34 **phrase** describe   36 **that former
fabulous story** so that stories formerly thought incredible

Being now seen possible enough, got credit,
That Bevis° was believed.

Buckingham.　　　　　　　　O, you go far.

Norfolk. As I belong to worship,° and affect
In honor honesty,° the tract of everything　　　　　40
Would by a good discourser lose some life
Which action's self was tongue to.° All was royal;
To the disposing of it nought rebelled.°
Order gave each thing view;° the office° did
Distinctly° his full function.

Buckingham.　　　　　　　Who did guide—　　　　45
I mean, who set the body and the limbs
Of this great sport° together, as you guess?

Norfolk. One, certes,° that promises no element°
In such a business.

Buckingham.　　　I pray you, who, my lord?

Norfolk. All this was ord'red° by the good discretion　50
Of the right reverend Cardinal of York.

Buckingham. The devil speed him!° No man's pie
　　is freed
From his ambitious finger. What had he
To do in these fierce° vanities? I wonder
That such a keech° can with his very bulk　　　　55
Take up° the rays o' th' beneficial sun,°
And keep it from the earth.

---

38 **Bevis** Bevis of Hampton, the legendary Saxon knight celebrated in medieval romance　39 **worship** the nobility　39–40 **affect/In honor honesty** love truth as a point of honor　40–42 **the tract . . . tongue to** the course of all these events, however well narrated, would in the description lose some of the color and spark of the actuality　43 **rebelled** jarred　44 **Order gave each thing view** everything was arranged so that it could easily be viewed　44 **office** official, or officials as a group　45 **Distinctly** i.e., without confusion　47 **sport** entertainment　48 **certes** certainly　48 **promises no element** would not be expected to share　50 **ord'red** arranged　52 **The devil speed him** the Devil, i.e. rather than God, prosper him　54 **fierce** extravagant　55 **keech** animal fat rolled into a lump (with a sneer at Wolsey's reputed origin as a butcher's son; cf. line 120)　56 **Take up** obstruct　56 **sun** i.e., the King

Norfolk.   Surely, sir,
There's in him stuff° that puts him to these ends;
For, being not propped by ancestry, whose grace
60 Chalks successors their way,° nor called upon
For high feats done to th' crown,° neither allied
To eminent assistants,° but spider-like,
Out of his self-drawing° web, 'a gives us note,°
The force of his own merit makes his way°—
65 A gift° that heaven gives for him, which buys
A place next to the King.

Abergavenny.   I cannot tell
What heaven hath given him: let some graver eye
Pierce into that. But I can see his pride
Peep through each part of him. Whence has he
        that?
70 If not from hell, the devil is a niggard,°
Or has given all before, and he begins
A new hell in himself.

Buckingham.   Why the devil,
Upon this French going out,° took he upon him
(Without the privity° o' th' King) t' appoint
75 Who should attend on him? He makes up the file°
Of all the gentry, for the most part such
To whom as great a charge° as little honor
He meant to lay upon; and his own letter,
The honorable board of council out,°
Must fetch him in he papers.°

80 *Abergavenny.*   I do know
Kinsmen of mine, three at the least, that have

---

58 **stuff** qualities, capabilities   59–60 **whose grace . . . way** whose
special excellence marks a path for followers   60–61 **called . . .
crown** chosen in recognition of lofty exploits in behalf of the crown
62 **assistants** (1) public officials (2) supporters   63 **self-drawing**
self-spinning   63 **'a gives us note** he lets us know   64 **makes his
way** wins him preferment   65 **gift** i.e., merit   70 **If not . . . niggard**
(the devil is the source of pride, the sin for which Lucifer fell and
hell was created)   73 **going out** expedition   74 **privity** confiden-
tial participation   75 **file** list   77 **charge** expense   79 **out** uncon-
sulted   80 **fetch him in he papers** fetch in whom he puts on his list

By this so sickened their estates that never
They shall abound° as formerly.

Buckingham.   O, many
Have broke their backs with laying manors on 'em°
For this great journey. What did this vanity°   85
But minister communication of
A most poor issue?°

Norfolk.   Grievingly I think,
The peace between the French and us not values°
The cost that did conclude it.

Buckingham.   Every man,
After the hideous storm that followed, was   90
A thing inspired, and, not consulting,° broke
Into a general prophecy:° that this tempest,
Dashing the garment of this peace, aboded°
The sudden breach on't.

Norfolk.   Which is budded out;
For France hath flawed the league, and hath at-
    tached°   95
Our merchants' goods at Bordeaux.

Abergavenny.   Is it therefore
Th' ambassador is silenced?

Norfolk.   Marry,° is't.

Abergavenny. A proper title of a peace,° and pur-
    chased
At a superfluous rate!°

Buckingham.   Why, all this business
Our reverend Cardinal carried.°

83 **abound** prosper   84 **broke . . . manors on 'em** ruined themselves
by pawning their estates to outfit themselves   85 **vanity** extrava-
gance   86–87 **minister . . . issue** furnish occasion for unproductive
talk (with a possible quibble, "poor issue" = impoverished heirs)
88 **not values** is not worth   91 **not consulting** i.e., one another   92
a general prophecy i.e., all prophesied the same   93 **aboded** foretold
95 **flawed the league, and hath attached** broken the treaty and
confiscated   97 **Marry** (a mild oath, from the name of the Virgin
Mary)   98 **A proper title of a peace** an excellent contract of peace
(ironic)   99 **superfluous rate** excessive cost   100 **carried** managed

100 *Norfolk.*   Like it° your Grace,
      The state takes notice of the private difference°
      Betwixt you and the Cardinal. I advise you
      (And take it from a heart that wishes towards you
      Honor and plenteous° safety) that you read°
105   The Cardinal's malice and his potency°
      Together; to consider further that
      What his high hatred would effect wants not
      A minister° in his power. You know his nature,
      That he's revengeful, and I know his sword
110   Hath a sharp edge. It's long and 't may be said
      It reaches far, and where 'twill not extend,°
      Thither he darts it. Bosom up° my counsel;
      You'll find it wholesome.° Lo, where comes that
        rock
      That I advise your shunning.

Enter Cardinal Wolsey, the purse° borne before him,
certain of the Guard, and two Secretaries with papers.
The Cardinal in his passage fixeth his eye on Buck-
ingham, and Buckingham on him, both full of disdain.

115 *Wolsey.* The Duke of Buckingham's surveyor,° ha?
      Where's his examination?°

First Secretary.   Here, so please you.

Wolsey. Is he in person ready?

First Secretary.   Aye, please your Grace.

Wolsey. Well, we shall then know more, and Buck-
        ingham
      Shall lessen this big° look.
                              Exeunt Cardinal and his train.

100 **Like it** if it please (a courteous formula for volunteering un-
asked information)   101 **difference** disagreement   104 **plenteous**
ample   104 **read** construe   105 **potency** power   107–08 **wants not/**
A minister does not lack an agent   111 **extend** reach   112 **Bosom**
up conceal within your bosom   113 **wholesome** sound   114s.d.
purse bag containing the Great Seal that is the insignia of the Lord
Chancellor's office   115 **surveyor** overseer of an estate; Charles
Knyvet, Buckingham's cousin   116 **examination** deposition   119
big haughty

Buckingham. This butcher's cur° is venomed-mouthed,
　and I　　　　　　　　　　　　　　　　　　　　　　　　120
Have not the power to muzzle him. Therefore best
Not wake him in his slumber. A beggar's book
Outworths a noble's blood.°

Norfolk.　　　　　　　　　　What, are you chafed?°
Ask God for temp'rance; that's th' appliance only°
Which your disease requires.

Buckingham.　　　　　　　　　　I read in's looks　　125
Matter against me, and his eye reviled
Me as his abject object.° At this instant
He bores° me with some trick. He's gone to th' King;
I'll follow and outstare him.

Norfolk.　　　　　　　　　　Stay, my lord,
And let your reason with your choler question°　　130
What 'tis you go about. To climb steep hills
Requires slow pace at first. Anger is like
A full hot° horse who, being allowed his way,
Self-mettle° tires him. Not a man in England
Can advise me like you; be to yourself　　135
As you would to your friend.

Buckingham.　　　　　　　　　　I'll to the King,
And from a mouth of honor° quite cry down
This Ipswich° fellow's° insolence, or proclaim
There's difference in no persons.°

Norfolk.　　　　　　　　　　Be advised.°
Heat not a furnace for your foe so hot　　140
That it do singe yourself. We may outrun
By violent swiftness that which we run at,

---

120 **butcher's cur** (referring to Wolsey's parentage) 122–23 **A beggar's . . . blood** a beggar's book-learning is more esteemed than nobility of descent 123 **chafed** angry 124 **appliance only** only remedy 127 **abject object** object of contempt 128 **bores** cheats 130 **with your choler question** dispute with your anger 133 **full hot** high-spirited 134 **Self-mettle** his own natural vigor 137 **from a mouth of honor** speaking as a nobleman 138 **Ipswich** (Wolsey's birthplace) 138 **fellow's** (usually applied to inferiors; cf. III.ii.279 and IV.ii.100) 139 **There's . . . persons** distinctions of rank no longer matter 139 **Be advised** take care

And lose by overrunning.° Know you not
The fire that mounts the liquor° till't run o'er
145   In seeming to augment it wastes it? Be advised.
I say again there is no English soul
More stronger° to direct you than yourself,
If with the sap° of reason you would quench,
Or but allay, the fire of passion.

Buckingham.   Sir,
150   I am thankful to you, and I'll go along
By your prescription; but this top-proud° fellow
(Whom from the flow of gall I name not, but
From sincere motions)° by intelligence°
And proofs as clear as founts in July° when
155   We see each grain of gravel, I do know
To be corrupt and treasonous.

Norfolk.   Say not "treasonous."

Buckingham. To th' King I'll say't, and make my
          vouch° as strong
As shore of rock. Attend.° This holy fox,
Or wolf, or both (for he is equal rav'nous
160   As he is subtle, and as prone to mischief
As able to perform't, his mind and place°
Infecting one another, yea, reciprocally)
Only to show his pomp° as well in France
As here at home, suggests° the King our master
165   To this last costly treaty, th' interview,°
That swallowed so much treasure, and like a glass
Did break i' th' wrenching.°

---

143 **overrunning** running beyond   144 **mounts the liquor** causes the
liquor to rise   147 **More stronger** better qualified (double com-
paratives, and also superlatives, are frequent in Shakespeare)   148
sap juice, fluid   151 **top-proud** excessively proud   152–53 **Whom
. . . motions** of whom I thus speak not out of spite but from sincere
motives   153 **intelligence** intelligence reports   154 **founts in July**
i.e., streams no longer muddied by spring floods (the accent in "July"
is on the first syllable)   157 **vouch** allegation   158 **Attend** listen
161 **mind and place** inclinations and position   163 **pomp** magnificence   164 **suggests** prompts (used of the devil)   165 **interview** "ceremonial meeting of princes" (Foakes)   167 **wrenching**
rinsing

Norfolk.   Faith, and so it did.

Buckingham. Pray give me favor,° sir. This cunning
        Cardinal
    The articles o' th' combination drew°
    As himself pleased; and they were ratified   170
    As he cried, "Thus let be," to as much end
    As give a crutch to th' dead. But our count-cardinal
    Has done this, and 'tis well; for worthy Wolsey,
    Who cannot err, he did it. Now this follows
    (Which, as I take it, is a kind of puppy   175
    To th' old dam,° treason) Charles the Emperor,
    Under pretense to see the Queen his aunt
    (For 'twas indeed his color,° but he came
    To whisper Wolsey) here makes visitation.°
    His fears were that the interview betwixt   180
    England and France might through their amity
    Breed him some prejudice, for from this league
    Peeped harms that menaced him. He privily°
    Deals with our Cardinal; and, as I trow°
    (Which I do well, for I am sure the Emperor   185
    Paid ere he promised, whereby his suit was granted
    Ere it was asked) but when the way was made
    And paved with gold, the Emperor thus desired,
    That he would please to alter the King's course
    And break the foresaid peace. Let the King know,   190
    As soon he shall by me, that thus the Cardinal
    Does buy and sell° his honor as he pleases,
    And for his own advantage.

Norfolk.   I am sorry
    To hear this of him, and could wish he were
    Something mistaken° in't.

Buckingham.   No, not a syllable: 195

168 **Pray give me favor** please hear me out   169 **articles o' th'
combination drew** drew up the terms of the peace treaty   176 **dam**
mother   178 **color** pretext   179 **makes visitation** pays a visit   183
privily secretly   184 **as I trow** as I believe (the principal clause
required after the parenthetical comment does not appear; grammar has yielded to the speaker's emotion, but the sense of the
passage is clear)   192 **buy and sell** traffic in   195 **Something
mistaken** to some extent misinterpreted

I do pronounce° him in that very shape
He shall appear in proof.°

*Enter Brandon, a Sergeant-at-Arms before him, and
two or three of the Guard.*

Brandon. Your office, sergeant: execute it.

Sergeant.   Sir,
My lord the Duke of Buckingham, and Earl
200 Of Hereford, Stafford, and Northampton, I
Arrest thee of high treason, in the name
Of our most sovereign King.

Buckingham.   Lo you,° my lord,
The net has fall'n upon me! I shall perish
Under device and practice.°

Brandon.   I am sorry
205 To see you ta'en from liberty, to look on
The business present.° 'Tis his Highness' pleasure
You shall to th' Tower.°

Buckingham.   It will help me nothing
To plead mine innocence, for that dye is on me
Which makes my whit'st part black. The will of
heav'n
210 Be done in this and all things! I obey.
O my Lord Aberga'ny, fare you well!

Brandon. Nay, he must bear you company.
  [*To Abergavenny*] The King
Is pleased you shall to th' Tower, till you know
How he determines further.

Abergavenny.   As the Duke said,
215 The will of heaven be done, and the King's pleasure
By me obeyed!

Brandon.   Here is a warrant from

196 **pronounce** declare   197 **He shall appear in proof** experience
will reveal him   202 **Lo you** behold   204 **device and practice**
plots and intrigues   205–06 **to look . . . present** (1) and to see
what is now happening (2) to be involved in the present affair   207
Tower the Tower of London (where suspected traitors were im-
prisoned)

The King t' attach° Lord Montacute, and the bodies°
Of the Duke's confessor, John de la Car,
One Gilbert Parke, his councillor—

Buckingham.   So, so;
These are the limbs o' th' plot. No more, I hope. *220*

Brandon. A monk o' th' Chartreux.°

Buckingham.   O, Nicholas Hopkins?

Brandon.   He.

Buckingham. My surveyor is false; the o'er-great
    Cardinal
Hath showed him gold. My life is spanned° already.
I am the shadow of poor Buckingham,
Whose figure even this instant cloud puts on,   *225*
By dark'ning my clear sun.° My lord, farewell.
                                        Exeunt.

Scene II. [*The same. The council-chamber.*]

*Cornets. Enter King Henry, leaning on the Cardinal's
shoulder; the Nobles, [a Secretary of the Cardinal's,]
and Sir Thomas Lovell. The Cardinal places himself
under the King's feet° on his right side.*

King. My life itself, and the best heart° of it,
Thanks you for this great care. I stood i' th' level°
Of a full-charged confederacy,° and give thanks
To you that choked it. Let be called before us

217 **attach** arrest 217 **bodies** persons 221 **Chartreux** Charter-
house (i.e., a Carthusian) 223 **spanned** measured out 225–26
Whose figure . . . sun whose form is at this instant clouded by misfortune that dims my glory and alienates me from my King ("sun"
may refer to both Buckingham and Henry) I.ii.s.d. **under the King's
feet** at the feet of the King, who is seated on a raised and canopied
"state," or throne 1 **best heart** very core 2 **i' th' level** in direct
range 3 **full-charged confederacy** fully-loaded conspiracy

5   That gentleman of Buckingham's.° In person
     I'll hear him his confessions justify,°
     And point by point the treasons of his master
     He shall again relate.

     A noise within, crying "Room for the Queen!"
     [*Katherine, who is*] *ushered by the Duke of Norfolk.*
     Enter the Queen, [*Duke of*] *Norfolk and* [*Duke of*]
     Suffolk. She kneels. King riseth from his state, takes
     her up, kisses and placeth her by him.

     Queen Katherine. Nay, we must longer kneel: I am
        a suitor.

10   *King.* Arise, and take place° by us. Half your suit
     Never name to us: you have half our power.
     The other moiety° ere you ask is given.
     Repeat your will,° and take it.

     Queen Katherine.   Thank your Majesty.
     That you would love yourself, and in that love
15   Not unconsiderèd leave your honor nor
     The dignity of your office, is the point
     Of my petition.

     King.   Lady mine, proceed.

     Queen Katherine. I am solicited,° not by a few,
     And those of true condition,° that your subjects
20   Are in great grievance. There have been commissions
     Sent down among 'em, which hath flawed° the heart
     Of all their loyalties; wherein although,
     My good Lord Cardinal, they vent reproaches
     Most bitterly on you as putter-on°
25   Of these exactions, yet the King our master—
     Whose honor heaven shield from soil!—even he
        escapes not
     Language unmannerly; yea, such which breaks

5 **That gentleman of Buckingham's** (the surveyor referred to at
I.i.222) 6 **justify** confirm 10 **take place** be seated 12 **moiety** half
13 **Repeat your will** state your wish 18 **solicited** informed by peti-
tioners 19 **true condition** loyal disposition 21 **flawed** broken 24
putter-on instigator

The sides of loyalty, and almost appears
In loud rebellion.

Norfolk.   Not almost appears—
It doth appear. For, upon these taxations,   30
The clothiers all, not able to maintain
The many to them 'longing,° have put off
The spinsters, carders, fullers,° weavers, who,
Unfit for other life, compelled by hunger
And lack of other means, in desperate manner   35
Daring th' event to th' teeth,° are all in uproar,
And danger serves among them.°

King.   Taxation?
Wherein? And what taxation? My Lord Cardinal,
You that are blamed for it alike with us,
Know you of this taxation?

Wolsey.   Please you, sir,   40
I know but of a single part° in aught
Pertains to th' state, and front but in that file
Where others tell steps with me.°

Queen Katherine.   No, my lord?
You know no more than others? But you frame
Things that are known alike,° which are not whole-
some   45
To° those which would not know them, and yet must
Perforce be their acquaintance.° These exactions
(Whereof my sovereign would have note),° they
are
Most pestilent° to th' hearing; and to bear 'em
The back is sacrifice to th' load. They say   50

---

32 **to them 'longing** employed by them   33 **spinsters, carders, fullers** "spinsters" = spinners (usually female); carders combed out impurities from the wool; fullers cleansed the cloth by beating 36 **Daring th' event to th' teeth** defiantly daring the worst   37 **serves among them** is welcomed as a comrade   41 **a single part** i.e., my own individual share   42–43 **front ... with me** only march in the front rank of those who keep in step with me, i.e., share my responsibility   44–45 **frame ... alike** devise measures known to all alike (in the council)   45–46 **wholesome/To** (1) beneficial to (2) approved by   47 **their acquaintance** acquainted with them   48 **note** knowledge   49 **pestilent** offensive

They are devised by you, or else you suffer
Too hard an exclamation.°

King.   Still exaction!
The nature of it? In what kind, let's know,
Is this exaction?

Queen Katherine. I am much too venturous
55   In tempting of your patience, but am boldened
Under your promised pardon. The subject's grief°
Comes through commissions, which compels from
         each
The sixth part of his substance, to be levied
Without delay; and the pretense° for this
Is named your wars in France. This makes bold
60   mouths.
Tongues spit their duties out, and cold hearts freeze
Allegiance° in them. Their curses now
Live where their prayers did, and it's come to pass,
This tractable obedience is a slave
65   To each incensèd will.° I would your Highness
Would give it quick consideration, for
There is no primer baseness.°

King.   By my life,
This is against our pleasure.

Wolsey.   And for me,
I have no further gone in this than by
70   A single voice,° and that not passed me but
By learned approbation of the judges. If I am
Traduced by ignorant tongues, which neither know
My faculties° nor person, yet will be
The chronicles of my doing, let me say
75   'Tis but the fate of place,° and the rough brake°
That virtue must go through. We must not stint
Our necessary actions in the fear

---

52 **exclamation** reproach   56 **grief** grievance   59 **pretense** pretext
62 **Allegiance** (four syllables)   64–65 **This tractable . . . will** this
willing obedience of theirs has given way to angry passion   67
primer baseness "mischief more urgently in need of redress"
(Foakes)   70 **voice** vote   73 **faculties** qualities   75 **place** high office   75 **brake** thicket

To cope° malicious censurers, which ever,
As rav'nous fishes, do a vessel follow
That is new-trimmed,° but benefit no further   80
Than vainly longing. What we oft do best,
By sick° interpreters (once° weak ones) is
Not ours or not allowed;° what worst, as oft,
Hitting a grosser quality,° is cried up
For our best act. If we shall stand still,   85
In fear our motion° will be mocked or carped at,
We should take root here where we sit,
Or sit state-statues only.°

King.   Things done well,
And with a care, exempt themselves from fear.
Things done without example,° in their issue°   90
Are to be feared. Have you a precedent
Of this commission? I believe, not any.
We must not rend° our subjects from our laws,
And stick them in our will.° Sixth part of each?
A trembling° contribution! Why, we take   95
From every tree lop,° bark, and part o' th' timber,
And though we leave it with a root, thus hacked,°
The air will drink the sap. To every county
Where this is questioned° send our letters with
Free pardon to each man that has denied   100
The force° of this commission. Pray look to't;
I put it to your care.

Wolsey.   [*To the Secretary*] A word with you.
Let there be letters writ to every shire
Of the King's grace and pardon. The grievèd com-
      mons

---

78 **cope** encounter   80 **new-trimmed** newly made seaworthy   82
sick unsound   82 **once** in short   83 **Not ours or not allowed** denied
us or condemned   84 **Hitting a grosser quality** appealing to the baser
sort   86 **motion** (1) movement (2) proposal   88 **state-statues only**
mere replicas of statesmen   90 **example** precedent   90 **issue** consequences   93 **rend** pluck   94 **stick them in our will** i.e., make them
creatures of our arbitrary power   95 **trembling** accompanied by,
or causing, trembling   96 **lop** smaller branches and twigs   97 **thus
hacked** when it is thus hacked   99 **questioned** disputed   101 **force**
validity

105 Hardly conceive° of me: let it be noised
That through our° intercession this revokement
And pardon comes. I shall anon° advise you
Further in the proceeding.   *Exit Secretary.*

Enter Surveyor.

Queen Katherine. I am sorry that the Duke of
        Buckingham
Is run in° your displeasure.

110 *King.*   It grieves many.
The gentleman is learned and a most rare° speaker;
To nature none more bound;° his training such
That he may furnish and instruct great teachers,
And never seek for aid out of° himself. Yet see,
115 When these so noble benefits° shall prove
Not well disposed,° the mind growing once corrupt,
They turn to vicious forms, ten times more ugly
Than ever they were fair. This man so complete,
Who was enrolled 'mongst wonders, and when we,
120 Almost with ravished listening,° could not find
His hour of speech a minute—he, my lady,
Hath into monstrous habits° put the graces
That once were his, and is become as black
As if besmeared in hell. Sit by us. You shall hear—
125 This was his gentleman in trust°—of him
Things to strike honor sad. Bid him recount
The fore-recited practices,° whereof
We cannot feel too little, hear too much.

Wolsey. Stand forth, and with bold spirit relate what°
        you,
130 Most like a careful subject, have collected°
Out of the Duke of Buckingham.

---

105 **Hardly conceive** (1) think harshly (2) scarcely have any conception 106 **our** (note his use of the royal pronoun) 107 **anon**
soon 110 **Is run in** has incurred 111 **rare** accomplished 112
bound indebted (for his endowments) 114 **out of** from outside
115 **benefits** natural gifts 116 **disposed** applied 120 **Almost with
ravished listening** listening almost spellbound 122 **habits** garments
125 **in trust** trusted 127 **fore-recited practices** already revealed
plots 129 **what** i.e., what information 130 **collected** gathered (by
spying)

King.   Speak freely.

Surveyor. First, it was usual with him—every day
It would infect his speech—that if the King
Should without issue die, he'll carry it° so
To make the scepter his. These very words   135
I've heard him utter to his son-in-law,
Lord Aberga'ny, to whom by oath he menaced
Revenge upon the Cardinal.

Wolsey.   Please your Highness, note
This dangerous conception° in this point.
Not friended by his wish,° to your high person   140
His will is most malignant, and it stretches
Beyond you to your friends.

Queen Katherine.   My learned Lord Cardinal,
Deliver all with charity.

King.   Speak on.
How grounded he his title to the crown
Upon our fail?° To this point hast thou heard him   145
At any time speak aught?

Surveyor.   He was brought to this
By a vain prophecy of Nicholas Henton.°

King. What was that Henton?

Surveyor.   Sir, a Chartreux friar,
His confessor, who fed him every minute
With words of sovereignty.°

King.   How know'st thou this?   150

Surveyor. Not long before your Highness sped to°
        France,
The Duke being at the Rose,° within the parish
Saint Lawrence Poultney, did of me demand

134 **carry it** manage things   139 **conception** design   140 **Not friended
by his wish** not granted his wish (that the King should die child-
less)   145 **fail** (1) failure to beget an heir (2) death   147 **Henton**
(his name was in fact Nicholas Hopkins, Henton being the name
of his priory)   150 **sovereignty** i.e., relating to his accession to the
throne   151 **sped to** set out for   152 **the Rose** a manor house
belonging to Buckingham

What was the speech° among the Londoners
155   Concerning the French journey. I replied
Men feared the French would prove perfidious,
To the King's danger. Presently° the Duke
Said 'twas the fear indeed and that he doubted°
'Twould prove the verity of certain words
160   Spoke by a holy monk "that oft," says he,
"Hath sent to me, wishing me to permit
John de la Car, my chaplain, a choice° hour
To hear from him a matter of some moment;
Whom after under the confession's seal
165   He solemnly had sworn that what he spoke
My chaplain to no creature living but
To me should utter, with demure° confidence
This pausingly ensued: 'Neither the King nor's heirs
(Tell you the Duke) shall prosper. Bid him strive
170   To win the love o' th' commonalty.° The Duke
Shall govern England.' "

Queen Katherine.   If I know you well,
You were the Duke's surveyor, and lost your office
On the complaint o' th' tenants. Take good heed
You charge not in your spleen° a noble person,
175   And spoil° your nobler soul.° I say, take heed;
Yes, heartily beseech you.

King.   Let him on.
Go forward.

Surveyor.   On my soul, I'll speak but truth.
I told my lord the Duke, by th' devil's illusions
The monk might be deceived, and that 'twas
    dangerous
180   To ruminate on this so far, until
It forged him° some design, which,° being believed,
It was much like to do. He answered, "Tush,

---

154 **speech** report   157 **Presently** instantly   158 **doubted** suspected
162 **choice** suitable   167 **demure** solemn   170 **commonalty** common people   174 **spleen** malice   175 **spoil** destroy   175 **nobler soul**
(moral nobility taking precedence over the nobility of rank mentioned in the previous line)   181 **forged him** caused him to fashion
181 **which** i.e., the monk's words

It can do me no damage"; adding further,
That, had the King in his last sickness failed,°
The Cardinal's and Sir Thomas Lovell's heads   185
Should have gone off.

King.   Ha! What, so rank?° Ah, ha!
There's mischief in this man. Canst thou say
    further?

Surveyor. I can, my liege.

King.   Proceed.

Surveyor.   Being at Greenwich,
After your Highness had reproved the Duke
About Sir William Bulmer—

King.   I remember   190
Of such a time: being my sworn° servant,
The Duke retained him his. But on. What hence?

Surveyor. "If" (quoth he), "I for this had been
    committed,
As to the Tower I thought, I would have played
The part my father meant to act upon   195
Th' usurper Richard, who, being at Salisbury,
Made suit to come in's presence; which if granted,
As he made semblance° of his duty, would
Have put his knife into him."

King.   A giant traitor!

Wolsey. Now, madam, may his Highness live in
    freedom,   200
And this man out of prison?

Queen Katherine.   God mend all!

King. There's something more would out of thee.
What say'st?

Surveyor. After "the Duke his father," with the
    "knife,"

---

184 **failed** died   186 **rank** (1) corrupt (2) full grown (the plot)
191 **sworn** (two syllables)   198 **semblance** pretense

He stretched him,° and with one hand on his
    dagger,
205 Another spread on's breast, mounting° his eyes,
He did discharge a horrible oath whose tenor
Was, were he evil used,° he would outgo
His father by as much as a performance
Does an irresolute° purpose.

King.   There's his period,°
210 To sheathe his knife in us. He is attached.°
Call him to present° trial. If he may
Find mercy in the law, 'tis his; if none,
Let him not seek't of us. By day and night!
He's traitor to th' height.°

                            Exeunt.

Scene III. [*An antechamber in the palace.*]

Enter Lord Chamberlain and Lord Sands.

Chamberlain. Is't possible the spells of France should
    juggle
Men into such strange mysteries?°

Sands.   New customs,
Though they be never so ridiculous
(Nay, let 'em be unmanly) yet are followed.

5 *Chamberlain.* As far as I see, all the good our English
Have got by the late voyage is but merely
A fit or two o' th' face;° but they are shrewd° ones,
For when they hold 'em,° you would swear directly

---

204 **stretched him** i.e., stretched himself to his full height 205
mounting raising 207 **evil used** badly treated 209 **irresolute** un-
fulfilled 209 **period** goal 210 **attached** arrested 211 **present** im-
mediate 214 **height** utmost degree I.iii.1–2 **juggle . . . mysteries** trick men into such oddly mysterious behavior 7 **A fit or
two o' th' face** a grimace or two 7 **shrewd** nasty 8 **hold 'em** i.e.,
screw up their faces in this way

Their very noses had been counsellors
To Pepin or Clotharius,° they keep state° so.   *10*

Sands. They have all new legs,° and lame ones; one
        would take it,
That never saw 'em pace° before, the spavin
Or springhalt° reigned among 'em.

Chamberlain.   Death! My lord,
    Their clothes are after such a pagan cut to't,°
    That, sure, th' have worn out Christendom.°   *15*

            Enter Sir Thomas Lovell.

                                        How now?
    What news, Sir Thomas Lovell?

Lovell.   Faith, my lord,
    I hear of none but the new proclamation
    That's clapped° upon the court gate.

Chamberlain.   What is't for?

Lovell. The reformation of our traveled gallants
    That fill the court with quarrels, talk, and tailors.   *20*

Chamberlain. I'm glad 'tis there. Now I would pray
        our monsieurs
    To think an English courtier may be wise,
    And never see the Louvre.°

Lovell.   They must either
    (For so run the conditions) leave those remnants
    Of fool and feather° that they got in France,   *25*
    With all their honorable points of ignorance°
    Pertaining thereunto, as fights and fireworks,°

10 **Pepin or Clotharius** sixth- and seventh-century Kings of the
Franks   10 **keep state** affect grandeur   11 **new legs** new fashions
in walking or bowing   12 **pace** walk (suggesting horse references
that follow)   12–13 **spavin/Or springhalt** diseases affecting horses'
legs   14 **to't** as well   15 **worn out Christendom** used up Christian
fashions   18 **clapped** fastened   23 **Louvre** palace of the French
kings in Paris; now the art museum   25 **fool and feather** foolish
fashions (alluding to the feathers worn by some gallants in their
hats)   26 **honorable points of ignorance** ignorant conceptions of
honorable conduct   27 **fights and fireworks** i.e., duelling and whor-
ing (with a possible reference to venereal disease as the outcome)

Abusing° better men than they can be
Out of a foreign wisdom, renouncing clean
30   The faith they have in tennis and tall stockings,
Short blist'red° breeches, and those types° of travel,
And understand° again like honest men,
Or pack° to their old playfellows. There, I take it,
They may, *cum privilegio*,° "*oui*" away
35   The lag-end° of their lewdness, and be laughed at.

Sands. 'Tis time to give 'em physic,° their diseases
Are grown so catching.

Chamberlain.   What a loss our ladies
Will have of these trim vanities!°

Lovell.   Aye, marry,
There will be woe indeed, lords. The sly whoresons
40   Have got a speeding° trick to lay down ladies.
A French song and a fiddle has no fellow.°

Sands. The devil fiddle 'em! I am glad they are going,
For, sure, there's no converting of 'em. Now
An honest country lord, as I am, beaten
45   A long time out of play, may bring his plain-song,°
And have an hour of hearing; and, by'r lady,°
Held current music° too.

Chamberlain.   Well said, Lord Sands.
Your colt's tooth° is not cast yet?

Sands.   No, my lord,
Nor shall not while I have a stump.°

Chamberlain.   Sir Thomas,
Whither were you agoing?

---

28 **Abusing** (goes with "points of ignorance," and is not parallel
with "renouncing" in the next line which continues the thought indicated by "leave" in line 24)   31 **blist'red** puffed   31 **types**
insignia   32 **understand** comprehend things, in general (with a possible quibble on "stand under" [i.e., clothes])   33 **pack** clear out
34 **cum privilegio** with license   35 **lag-end** latter part   36 **physic**
medical treatment   38 **trim vanities** spruce fops   40 **speeding** ef-
fective   41 **fellow** equal   45 **plain-song** simple melody   46 **by'r
lady** i.e., by the Virgin Mary (a mild oath)   47 **Held current music** have it accepted as good music   48 **colt's tooth** i.e., youthful
lustiness   49 **stump** (with a bawdy double meaning)

Lovell.   To the Cardinal's.   50
Your lordship is a guest too.

Chamberlain.   O, 'tis true.
This night he makes a supper, and a great one,
To many lords and ladies. There will be
The beauty of this kingdom, I'll assure you.

Lovell. That churchman bears a bounteous mind
  indeed,   55
A hand as fruitful as the land that feeds us.
His dews fall everywhere.

Chamberlain.   No doubt he's noble.
He had a black° mouth that said other of him.

Sands. He may, my lord; has wherewithal. In him
Sparing° would show a worse sin than ill doctrine.   60
Men of his way° should be most liberal;
They are set here for examples.

Chamberlain.   True, they are so,
But few now give so great ones. My barge stays;
Your lordship shall along. Come, good Sir Thomas,
We shall be late else, which I would not be,   65
For I was spoke to,° with Sir Henry Guildford
This night to be comptrollers.°

Sands.   I am your lordship's. *Exeunt.*

---

58 **black** evil   60 **Sparing** frugality   61 **way** i.e., of life   66 **spoke
to** asked   67 **comptrollers** household officers in charge of the
festivities

Scene IV. [*A Hall in York Place.*]

Hautboys.° A small table under a state° for the Car-
dinal, a longer table for the guests. Then enter Anne
Bullen and divers other Ladies and Gentlemen as
guests, at one door; at another door, enter Sir Henry
Guildford.

Guildford. Ladies, a general welcome from his Grace
　　Salutes ye all. This night he dedicates
　　To fair content and you. None here, he hopes,
　　In all this noble bevy,° has brought with her
5　　One care abroad. He would have all as merry
　　As, first, good company, good wine, good welcome,
　　Can make good people.

　　　　　　　Enter Lord Chamberlain, Lord Sands, and
　　　　　　　　　　[Sir Thomas] Lovell.

　　　　　　　　　　　　O, my lord, y'are tardy.
　　The very thought of this fair company
　　Clapped wings to me.

Chamberlain. You are young, Sir Harry Guildford.

10　*Sands.* Sir Thomas Lovell, had the Cardinal
　　But half my lay thoughts in him, some of these
　　Should find a running banquet,° ere they rested,
　　I think would better please 'em. By my life,
　　They are a sweet society° of fair ones.

15　*Lovell.* O, that your lordship were but now confessor
　　To one or two of these!

Sands.　　　　　　　　I would I were;
　　They should find easy penance.

I.iv.s.d. **Hautboys** oboes　s.d. **state** canopy　4 **bevy** company (of
ladies)　12 **running banquet** hasty repast (with a bawdy double
meaning)　14 **society** assembly

Lovell.   Faith, how easy?

Sands. As easy as a down bed would afford it.

Chamberlain. Sweet ladies, will it please you sit? Sir
    Harry,
  Place you° that side; I'll take the charge of this.   *20*
  His Grace is ent'ring. Nay, you must not freeze.
  Two women placed together makes cold weather.
  My Lord Sands, you are one will keep 'em waking:
  Pray, sit between these ladies.

Sands.   By my faith,
  And thank your lordship. By your leave, sweet
    ladies.   *25*
  If I chance to talk a little wild, forgive me;
  I had it from my father.

Anne.   Was he mad, sir?

Sands. O, very mad, exceeding mad, in love too;
  But he would bite none. Just as I do now,
  He would kiss you twenty with a breath.°

                                [Kisses her.]

Chamberlain.   Well said,° my lord. *30*
  So, now y'are fairly° seated. Gentlemen,
  The penance lies on you if these fair ladies
  Pass away° frowning.

Sands.   For my little cure,°
  Let me alone.

    *Hautboys. Enter Cardinal Wolsey, and takes
        his state.°*

Wolsey. Y'are welcome, my fair guests. That noble
    lady   *35*
  Or gentleman that is not freely merry

---

20 **Place you** i.e., place the guests 30 **kiss you twenty with a
breath** kiss twenty in one breath 30 **said** done 31 **fairly** properly
33 **Pass away** leave 33 **cure** (1) charge, parish (continuing the ecclesiastical metaphor of lines 15ff.) (2) remedy 34s.d. **state** chair of
state

Is not my friend. This, to confirm my welcome;
And to you all, good health.   [*Drinks.*]

Sands.   Your Grace is noble.
Let me have such a bowl may hold my thanks,
And save me so much talking.

40 *Wolsey.*   My Lord Sands,
I am beholding° to you. Cheer your neighbors.
Ladies, you are not merry. Gentlemen,
Whose fault is this?

Sands.   The red wine first must rise
In their fair cheeks, my lord. Then we shall have
'em
Talk us to silence.

45 *Anne.*   You are a merry gamester,°
My Lord Sands.

Sands.   Yes, if I make my play.°
Here's to your ladyship; and pledge it, madam,
For 'tis to such a thing—

Anne.   You cannot show me.

Sands. I told your Grace they would talk anon.
            Drum and trumpet; chambers° discharged.

Wolsey.   What's that?

Chamberlain. Look out there, some° of ye.
                                        [*Exit Servant.*]

50 *Wolsey.*   What warlike voice,
And to what end, is this? Nay, ladies, fear not;
By all the laws of war y'are privileged.°

            [*Re-*]*enter a Servant.*

Chamberlain. How now, what is't?

Servant.   A noble troop of strangers,

---

41 **beholding** beholden   45 **gamester** playful person   46 **make my
play** win my game   49s.d. **chambers** small cannon used for ceremonial purposes   50 **some** some one (cf. also line 60)   52 **privileged**
entitled to immunity

For so they seem. Th' have left their barge, and
    landed,
And hither make,° as great ambassadors   55
From foreign princes.

Wolsey.   Good Lord Chamberlain,
    Go, give 'em welcome: you can speak the French
        tongue;
    And pray receive 'em nobly and conduct 'em
    Into our presence, where this heaven of beauty
    Shall shine at full upon them. Some attend him.   60
            [*Exit Chamberlain, attended.*] *All rise,
                        and tables removed.*
    You have now a broken° banquet, but we'll mend
        it.
    A good digestion to you all; and once more
    I show'r a welcome on ye: welcome all.

*Hautboys. Enter King and others, as masquers,°
habited° like shepherds, ushered by the Lord Chamberlain. They pass directly before the Cardinal, and
gracefully salute him.*

    A noble company! What are their pleasures?

Chamberlain. Because they speak no English,
    thus they prayed   65
    To tell your Grace: that, having heard by fame°
    Of this so noble and so fair assembly
    This night to meet here, they could do no less
    (Out of the great respect they bear to beauty)
    But leave their flocks and, under your fair conduct,°   70
    Crave leave to view these ladies and entreat
    An hour of revels with 'em.

Wolsey.   Say, Lord Chamberlain,
    They have done my poor house grace; for which I
        pay 'em

55 **make** make their way   61 **broken** interrupted, with a possible
pun on "poor remains" (of a feast)   63s.d. **masquers** i.e., disguised
and vizarded as for a court masque   63s.d. **habited** dressed   66
fame report   70 **under your fair conduct** with your kind permission

   A thousand thanks and pray 'em take their
      pleasures. *Choose ladies; King and Anne Bullen.*

75 *King.* The fairest hand I ever touched! O beauty,
      Till now I never knew thee!   *Music. Dance.*

Wolsey. My lord!

Chamberlain.   Your Grace?

Wolsey.   Pray tell 'em thus much from me:
      There should be one amongst 'em, by his person,
      More worthy this place than myself, to whom
80   (If I but knew him) with my love and duty
      I would surrender it.°

Chamberlain.   I will, my lord.
                        Whisper[s with the masquers].

Wolsey. What say they?

Chamberlain.   Such a one, they all confess,
      There is indeed, which they would have your Grace
      Find out, and he will take it.

Wolsey.   Let me see then.
85   By all your good leaves, gentlemen; here I'll make
      My royal choice.°

King. [*Unmasking*] Ye have found him, Cardinal.
      You hold a fair assembly; you do well, lord.
      You are a churchman, or, I'll tell you, Cardinal,
      I should judge now unhappily.°

Wolsey.   I am glad
      Your Grace is grown so pleasant.°

90 *King.*   My Lord Chamberlain,
      Prithee come hither. What fair lady's that?

Chamberlain. An't please your Grace, Sir Thomas
      Bullen's daughter,
      The Viscount Rochford, one of her Highness'
      women.

81 **it** i.e., the place of honor   86 **royal choice** choice of a king   89
unhappily unfavorably   90 **pleasant** merry

King. By heaven, she is a dainty one. Sweetheart,
　I were unmannerly to take you out°　　　　　　　*95*
　And not to kiss you.° A health, gentlemen!
　Let it go round.

Wolsey. Sir Thomas Lovell, is the banquet ready
　I' th' privy chamber?

Lovell.　　　　　　　　Yes, my lord.

Wolsey.　　　　　　　　　　　Your Grace,
　I fear, with dancing is a little heated.　　　　　*100*

King. I fear, too much.

Wolsey.　　　　　　There's fresher air, my lord,
　In the next chamber.

King. Lead in your ladies, every one. Sweet partner,
　I must not yet forsake you. Let's be merry,
　Good my Lord Cardinal. I have half a dozen healths　*105*
　To drink to these fair ladies, and a measure°
　To lead 'em once again; and then let's dream
　Who's best in favor.° Let the music knock it.°
　　　　　　　　　　　Exeunt with trumpets.

---

95 **to take you out** i.e., to invite you to dance　96 **to kiss you**
(customary following a dance)　106 **measure** stately dance　108
best in favor (1) prettiest (2) most favored (by the ladies)　108
knock it strike up

ACT II

Scene I. [*Westminster. A street.*]

Enter two Gentlemen at several° doors.

First Gentleman. Whither away so fast?

Second Gentleman.   O, God save ye!
Ev'n to the Hall,° to hear what shall become
Of the great Duke of Buckingham.

First Gentleman.   I'll save you
That labor, sir. All's now done but the ceremony
Of bringing back the prisoner.

5 **Second Gentleman.**   Were you there?

First Gentleman. Yes, indeed was I.

Second Gentleman.   Pray speak what has happened.

First Gentleman. You may guess quickly what.

Second Gentleman.   Is he found guilty?

First Gentleman. Yes, truly is he, and condemned
    upon't.

Second Gentleman. I am sorry for't.

First Gentleman.   So are a number more.

II.i.s.d. **several** different   **2 Hall** Westminster Hall

74

Second Gentleman. But, pray, how passed it?°   10

First Gentleman. I'll tell you in a little.° The great
  Duke
  Came to the bar, where to his accusations
  He pleaded still not guilty, and allegèd°
  Many sharp reasons to defeat° the law.
  The King's attorney° on the contrary°   15
  Urged on° the examinations, proofs,° confessions
  Of divers witnesses; which the Duke desired
  To him brought *viva voce* to his face;
  At which appeared against him his surveyor;
  Sir° Gilbert Parke, his councillor; and John Car,   20
  Confessor to him; with that devil monk,
  Hopkins, that made this mischief.

Second Gentleman.   That was he
  That fed him with his prophecies?

First Gentleman.   The same.
  All these accused him strongly, which° he fain°
  Would have flung from him; but indeed he could
    not.   25
  And so his peers upon this evidence
  Have found him guilty of high treason. Much
  He spoke, and learnedly, for life, but all
  Was either pitied in him or forgotten.°

Second Gentleman. After all this, how did he bear
  himself?   30

First Gentleman. When he was brought again to th'
  bar, to hear
  His knell rung out, his judgment,° he was stirred
  With such an agony he sweat extremely

---

10 **how passed it** i.e., what happened at the trial   11 **in a little**
in brief   13 **allegèd** put forward   14 **defeat** frustrate   15 **King's
attorney** John Fitz-James, afterward Chief Justice of the King's
Bench   15 **contrary** contrary side   16 **Urged on** (1) argued on the
evidence of (intransitive) (2) pressed the evidence of (transitive)
16 **examinations, proofs** depositions, statements   20 **Sir** (a courtesy title for a cleric)   24 **which** i.e., which accusations   24 **fain**
gladly   29 **Was . . . forgotten** either aroused only unavailing pity
or had no effect   32 **judgment** sentence (also in line 58)

And something spoke in choler, ill and hasty.
35 But he fell to himself again, and sweetly
In all the rest showed a most noble patience.

Second Gentleman. I do not think he fears death.

First Gentleman.   Sure,° he does not;
He never was so womanish. The cause
He may a little grieve at.

Second Gentleman.   Certainly
The Cardinal is the end° of this.

40 *First Gentleman.*   'Tis likely,
By all conjectures: first, Kildare's attainder,°
Then Deputy of Ireland, who removed,
Earl Surrey was sent thither, and in haste too,
Lest he should help his father.°

Second Gentleman.   That trick of state
Was a deep envious° one.

45 *First Gentleman.*   At his return
No doubt he will requite it. This is noted,
And generally:° whoever the King favors,
The Card'nal instantly will find employment,
And far enough from court too.

Second Gentleman.   All the commons
50 Hate him perniciously,° and, o' my conscience,
Wish him ten fathom deep. This Duke as much
They love and dote on; call him bounteous Buck-
     ingham,
The mirror of all courtesy—

Enter Buckingham from his arraignment, tipstaves°
before him, the ax with the edge towards him,
halberds° on each side, accompanied with Sir Thomas

---

37 Sure surely **40 the end** at the root **41 attainder** disgrace
44 father father-in-law (cf. III.ii.260–64) **45 envious** malicious
47 generally by all **50 perniciously** mortally **53s.d. tipstaves**
bailiffs, so called because they carried silver-tipped staffs **53s.d.**
halberds halberdiers (officers bearing long-handled weapons with
blade-and-spear points)

*Lovell, Sir Nicholas Vaux, Sir Walter Sands,° and
common people, etc.*

First Gentleman.   Stay there, sir,
And see the noble ruined man you speak of.

Second Gentleman. Let's stand close,° and behold him.

Buckingham.   All good people,   55
You that thus far have come to pity me,
Hear what I say, and then go home and lose° me.
I have this day received a traitor's judgment,
And by that name must die. Yet, heaven bear wit-
      ness,
And if I have a conscience, let it sink° me   60
Even as the ax falls, if I be not faithful!
The law I bear no malice for my death:
'T has done, upon the premises,° but justice.
But those that sought it I could wish more° Chris-
      tians.
Be what they will,° I heartily forgive 'em.   65
Yet let 'em look° they glory not in mischief
Nor build their evils° on the graves of great men,°
For then my guiltless blood must cry against 'em.
For further life in this world I ne'er hope,
Nor will I sue, although the King have mercies   70
More than I dare make faults. You few that loved
      me
And dare be bold to weep for Buckingham,
His noble friends and fellows, whom to leave
Is only bitter° to him, only dying,
Go with me like good angels to my end;   75
And as the long divorce of steel° falls on me,
Make of your prayers one sweet sacrifice,°
And lift my soul to heaven. Lead on, o' God's name.

53s.d. **Sir Walter Sands** (Sir William Sands in Holinshed) 55
close (1) out of view (2) silent   57 **lose** forget   60 **sink** destroy
63 **premises** (1) circumstances (2) proceedings   64 **more** i.e., more
sincere   65 **Be what they will** whoever they may be   66 **look** look
to it   67 **evils** privies (?)   67 **great men** noblemen   74 **only bitter**
the only bitterness   76 **divorce of steel** separation of body and soul
caused by the ax   77 **sacrifice** offering

Lovell. I do beseech your Grace, for charity,
80   If ever any malice in your heart
    Were hid against me, now to forgive me frankly.°

Buckingham. Sir Thomas Lovell, I as free forgive you
    As I would be forgiven. I forgive all.
    There cannot be those numberless offenses
    'Gainst me that I cannot take° peace with. No black
85   envy°
    Shall mark my grave. Commend me to his Grace,
    And if he speak of Buckingham, pray tell him
    You met him half in heaven. My vows and prayers
    Yet are the King's and, till my soul forsake,°
90   Shall cry for blessings on him. May he live
    Longer than I have time to tell° his years!
    Ever beloved and loving may his rule be,
    And when old time shall lead him to his end,
    Goodness and he fill up one monument!°

95 *Lovell.* To th' waterside I must conduct your Grace,
    Then give my charge up to Sir Nicholas Vaux,
    Who undertakes° you to your end.

Vaux.   Prepare there;
    The Duke is coming. See the barge be ready,
    And fit it with such furniture° as suits
    The greatness of his person.

100 *Buckingham.*   Nay, Sir Nicholas,
    Let it alone; my state now will but mock me.
    When I came hither, I was Lord High Constable
    And Duke of Buckingham; now, poor Edward
      Bohun.°
    Yet I am richer than my base accusers
105   That never knew what truth meant. I now seal° it,
    And with that blood will make 'em one day groan
      for't.

81 **frankly** freely (for Lovell's reference see I.ii.185–86)   85 **take** make   85 **envy** malice   89 **forsake** i.e., part from my body   91 **tell** count   94 **monument** grave   97 **undertakes** has charge of   99 **furniture** equipment   103 **Bohun** (his family name was actually Stafford, although in the female line he was descended from the Bohuns)   105 **seal** ratify

My noble father, Henry of Buckingham,
Who first raised head° against usurping Richard,°
Flying for succor to his servant Banister,
Being distressed, was by that wretch betrayed,   110
And without trial fell. God's peace be with him!
Henry the Seventh succeeding, truly pitying
My father's loss, like a most royal prince,
Restored me to my honors, and out of ruins
Made my name once more noble. Now his son,   115
Henry the Eighth, life, honor, name, and all
That made me happy, at one stroke has taken
Forever from the world. I had my trial,
And must needs say a noble one; which makes me
A little happier than my wretched father.   120
Yet thus far we are one in fortunes: both
Fell by our servants, by those men we loved most—
A most unnatural and faithless service!
Heaven has an end° in all. Yet, you that hear me,
This from a dying man receive as certain: 125
Where you are liberal of your loves and counsels
Be sure you be not loose.° For those you make
    friends
And give your hearts to, when they once perceive
The least rub° in your fortunes, fall away
Like water from ye, never found again   130
But where they mean to sink° ye. All good people,
Pray for me! I must now forsake ye; the last hour
Of my long weary life° is come upon me.
Farewell!
And when you would say something that is sad,   135
Speak how I fell. I have done, and God forgive me.
                    Exeunt Duke and Train.

First Gentleman. O, this is full of pity! Sir, it calls,
    I fear, too many curses on their heads
    That were the authors.°

Second Gentleman.   If the Duke be guiltless,

108 **raised head** gathered troops   108 **Richard** Richard III   124 **end**
purpose   127 **loose** careless   129 **rub** check   131 **sink** destroy
133 **long weary life** (he was forty-three)   139 **authors** originators

140   'Tis full of woe. Yet I can give you inkling
Of an ensuing evil, if it fall,
Greater than this.

First Gentleman.   Good angels keep it from us!
What may it be? You do not doubt my faith,° sir?

Second Gentleman. This secret is so weighty, 'twill require
A strong faith to conceal it.

145 First Gentleman.   Let me have it;
I do not talk much.

Second Gentleman.   I am confident;°
You shall,° sir. Did you not of late days hear
A buzzing° of a separation
Between the King and Katherine?

First Gentleman.   Yes, but it held°
not;
150   For when the King once heard it, out of anger
He sent command to the Lord Mayor straight
To stop the rumor and allay° those tongues
That durst disperse it.

Second Gentleman.   But that slander, sir,
Is found a truth now, for it grows again
155   Fresher than e'er it was, and held for certain
The King will venture at it. Either the Cardinal
Or some about him near have, out of malice
To the good Queen, possessed him with a scruple°
That will undo her. To confirm this too,
160   Cardinal Campeius is arrived, and lately;°
As all think, for this business.

First Gentleman.   'Tis the Cardinal;
And merely to revenge him on the Emperor°

143 **faith** trustworthiness   146 **confident** i.e., of your discretion
147 **shall** i.e., shall have it   148 **buzzing** rumor   149 **held** lasted
152 **allay** silence   158 **possessed him with a scruple** put a doubt in
his mind   160 **Cardinal . . . lately** (Lorenzo Campeggio, or Campeius, did not actually arrive from Rome until 1528, seven years
after Buckingham's execution)   162 **Emperor** (Charles V, Holy
Roman Emperor and King of Spain; nephew to Katherine. See
I.i.176–90 and II.ii.25)

For not bestowing on him at his asking
The archbishopric of Toledo, this is purposed.

Second Gentleman. I think you have hit the mark. But
    is't not cruel   *165*
That she should feel the smart of this? The Cardinal
Will have his will, and she must fall.

First Gentleman.   'Tis woeful.
We are too open° here to argue this;
Let's think in private more.

                               Exeunt.

Scene II. [*An antechamber in the palace.*]

    Enter Lord Chamberlain, reading this letter.

Chamberlain. "My lord, the horses your lordship sent
    for, with all the care I had, I saw well chosen,
    ridden,° and furnished.° They were young and hand-
    some, and of the best breed in the north. When they
    were ready to set out for London, a man of my   *5*
    Lord Cardinal's, by commission and main power,°
    took 'em from me, with this reason: his master
    would be served before a subject, if not before the
    King; which stopped our mouths, sir."
I fear he will indeed. Well, let him have them.   *10*
He will have all, I think.

    Enter to the Lord Chamberlain, the Dukes of
             Norfolk and Suffolk.

Norfolk. Well met, my Lord Chamberlain.

Chamberlain. Good day to both your Graces.

---

168 **open** (1) public (2) indiscreet   II.ii.3 **ridden** broken in   3
furnished outfitted   6 **commission and main power** warrant and
sheer force

Suffolk. How is the King employed?

Chamberlain.   I left him private,°
Full of sad° thoughts and troubles.

15 *Norfolk.*   What's the cause?

Chamberlain. It seems the marriage with his brother's
wife
Has crept too near his conscience.

Suffolk. [*Aside*]   No, his conscience
Has crept too near another lady.

Norfolk.   'Tis so.
This is the Cardinal's doing; the king-cardinal,
20 That blind priest, like the eldest son of Fortune,
Turns what he list.° The King will know° him one
day.

Suffolk. Pray God he do! He'll never know himself
else.

Norfolk. How holily he works in all his business,
And with what zeal! For, now he has cracked the
league
Between us and the Emperor, the Queen's great
25   nephew,
He dives into the King's soul, and there scatters
Dangers, doubts, wringing° of the conscience,
Fears and despairs; and all these for° his marriage.
And out of all these to restore the King,
30 He counsels a divorce, a loss of her
That like a jewel has hung twenty years
About his neck, yet never lost her luster;
Of her that loves him with that excellence
That angels love good men with, even of her
35 That, when the greatest stroke of fortune falls,
Will bless the King. And is not this course pious?

14 **private** alone   15 **sad** grave (also in lines 57, 62)   20–21 **That
blind . . . list** i.e., he takes after Fortune in his disregard for
others and his capriciousness (Fortune was depicted as blind and
turning a wheel; eldest sons had special privileges)   21 **know** understand (also in next line)   27 **wringing** torture   28 **for** because of

Chamberlain. Heaven keep me from such counsel! 'Tis
      most true
   These news are everywhere; every tongue speaks
      'em,
   And every true heart weeps for't. All that dare
   Look into these affairs see this main end,   40
   The French King's sister.° Heaven will one day
      open
   The King's eyes, that so long have slept upon°
   This bold bad man.

Suffolk.   And free us from his slavery.

Norfolk. We had need pray,
   And heartily, for our deliverance,   45
   Or this imperious man will work us all
   From princes into pages. All men's honors
   Lie like one lump° before him, to be fashioned
   Into what pitch° he please.

Suffolk.   For me, my lords,
   I love him not, nor fear him—there's my creed.   50
   As I am made without him, so I'll stand,
   If the King please. His curses and his blessings
   Touch me alike; th'are breath I not believe in.
   I knew him, and I know him; so I leave him
   To him that made him proud—the Pope.°

Norfolk.   Let's in,   55
   And with some other business put the King
   From these sad thoughts that work too much upon
      him.
   My lord, you'll bear us company?

Chamberlain.   Excuse me,
   The King has sent me otherwise. Besides,
   You'll find a most unfit time to disturb him.   60
   Health to your lordships.

---

41 The French King's sister the Duchess of Alençon (see III.ii.
85–86)   **42 slept upon** been blind to   **48 lump** i.e., of clay (cf.
Romans 9:21)   **49 pitch** height (figurative), i.e., rank or degree
of dignity   **55 the Pope** (the expected reference would be to the
devil)

Norfolk.   Thanks, my good Lord Chamberlain.

*Exit Lord Chamberlain, and the King draws
the curtain° and sits reading pensively.*

Suffolk. How sad he looks; sure, he is much afflicted.°

King. Who's there, ha?

Norfolk.   Pray God he be not angry.

King. Who's there, I say? How dare you thrust yourselves
65   Into my private meditations?
Who am I, ha?

Norfolk. A gracious king that pardons all offenses
Malice ne'er meant. Our breach of duty this way°
Is business of estate,° in which we come
To know your royal pleasure.

70 *King.*   Ye are too bold.
Go to;° I'll make ye know your times of business.
Is this an hour for temporal affairs, ha?

Enter Wolsey and Campeius, with a commission.

Who's there? My good Lord Cardinal? O my
Wolsey,
The quiet of my wounded conscience,
Thou art a cure fit for a king. [*To Campeius*] You're
75   welcome,
Most learnèd reverend sir, into our kingdom:
Use us and it. [*To Wolsey*] My good lord, have
great care
I be not found a talker.°

Wolsey.   Sir, you cannot.
I would your Grace would give us but an hour
Of private conference.

61s.d. **King draws the curtain** (he is thus revealed seated within
a curtained booth or recess; see Prefatory Remarks, p. xiv   62 **afflicted** disturbed   68 **this way** in this respect   69 **estate** state   71
Go to (an exclamation of impatience or disapproval)   78 **talker**
i.e., rather than a doer

King. [*To Norfolk and Suffolk*] We are busy; go.　　*80*

Norfolk. [*Aside to Suffolk*] This priest has no pride in
    him?

Suffolk. [*Aside to Norfolk*] Not to speak of.
 I would not be so sick though for his place.°
 But this cannot continue.

Norfolk. [*Aside to Suffolk*] If it do,
 I'll venture one have-at-him.°

Suffolk. [*Aside to Norfolk*]　　I another.
                Exeunt Norfolk and Suffolk.

Wolsey. Your Grace has given a precedent of wisdom　　*85*
 Above all princes, in committing freely
 Your scruple to the voice of Christendom.
 Who can be angry now? What envy° reach you?
 The Spaniard,° tied by blood and favor to her,
 Must now confess, if they have any goodness,　　*90*
 The trial just and noble. All the clerks°
 (I mean the learnèd ones) in Christian kingdoms
 Have their free voices.° Rome, the nurse of judg-
    ment,
 Invited by your noble self, hath sent
 One general tongue° unto us, this good man,　　*95*
 This just and learnèd priest, Card'nal Campeius,
 Whom once more I present unto your Highness.

King. And once more in mine arms I bid him welcome,
 And thank the holy conclave° for their loves.
 They have sent me such a man I would have wished
    for.　　*100*

Campeius. Your Grace must needs deserve all strang-
    ers'° loves,

82 so sick though for his place so sick with pride even if it meant
having his position　**84 have-at-him** thrust (the phrase "have at
you," meaning "here goes!" or "watch out!" signaled an attack)
88 envy malice　**89 Spaniard** Spaniards (Katherine was daughter
to Ferdinand of Spain)　**91 clerks** scholars　**93 Have their free
voices** may freely express their opinions　**95 One general tongue**
one spokesman for all　**99 holy conclave** College of Cardinals
101 strangers' foreigners'

You are so noble. To your Highness' hand
I tender my commission; by whose virtue,
The court of Rome commanding, you, my Lord
105 Cardinal of York, are joined with me their servant
In the unpartial° judging of this business.

King. Two equal° men. The Queen shall be acquainted
Forthwith for what you come. Where's Gardiner?

Wolsey. I know your Majesty has always loved her
110 So dear in heart not to deny her that°
A woman of less place might ask by law:
Scholars allowed freely to argue for her.

King. Aye, and the best she shall have, and my favor
To him that does best—God forbid else. Cardinal,
115 Prithee call Gardiner to me, my new secretary;
I find him a fit fellow.

                                        [*Wolsey beckons.*]

Enter Gardiner.

Wolsey. [*Aside to Gardiner*] Give me your hand:
    much joy and favor to you.
You are the King's now.

Gardiner. [*Aside to Wolsey*] But to be commanded
Forever by your Grace, whose hand has raised me.

120 *King.* Come hither, Gardiner.

Walks and whispers.

Campeius. My Lord of York, was not one Doctor
    Pace
In this man's place before him?

Wolsey.   Yes, he was.

Campeius. Was he not held a learnèd man?

Wolsey.   Yes, surely.

---

106 **unpartial** impartial   107 **equal** just, impartial   110 **that** that
which

Campeius. Believe me, there's an ill opinion spread
　　then,
　Even of yourself, Lord Cardinal.

Wolsey.　　　　　　　　　　　How? Of me?　　125

Campeius. They will not stick° to say you envied him
　And, fearing he would rise (he was so virtuous),
　Kept him a foreign man still;° which so grieved him
　That he ran mad and died.°

Wolsey.　　　　　　　　　Heaven's peace be with him!
　That's Christian care enough. For living murmurers°　130
　There's places of rebuke. He was a fool,
　For he would needs be virtuous. That good fellow,
　If I command him, follows my appointment;°
　I will have none so near else. Learn this, brother,
　We live not to be griped° by meaner persons.　　135

King. Deliver° this with modesty to th' Queen.
　　　　　　　　　　　　　　Exit Gardiner.
　The most convenient place that I can think of
　For such receipt° of learning is Blackfriars;°
　There ye shall meet about this weighty business.
　My Wolsey, see it furnished.° O, my lord,　　140
　Would it not grieve an able° man to leave
　So sweet a bedfellow? But, conscience, conscience!
　O, 'tis a tender place, and I must leave her.
　　　　　　　　　　　　　　　　Exeunt.

126 **stick** scruple　128 **a foreign man still** continually on missions abroad　129 **died** (Pace in fact outlived Wolsey by six years) 130 **murmurers** grumblers　133 **appointment** direction　135 **griped** clutched familiarly　136 **Deliver** relate　138 **receipt** accommodation　138 **Blackfriars** Dominican monastery buildings in London 140 **furnished** fitted up　141 **able** vigorous

Scene III. [*An antechamber of the Queen's apartments.*]

Enter Anne Bullen and an old Lady.

Anne. Not for that neither. Here's the pang that
　　pinches:°
　　His Highness having lived so long with her, and she
　　So good a lady that no tongue could ever
　　Pronounce° dishonor of her—by my life,
5　　She never knew harmdoing—O, now, after
　　So many courses of the sun° enthronèd,
　　Still growing in a majesty and pomp, the which
　　To leave a thousandfold more bitter than
　　'Tis sweet at first t' acquire—after this process,°
10　　To give her the avaunt,° it is a pity
　　Would move a monster.

Old Lady.　　　　　　　Hearts of most hard temper
　　Melt and lament for her.

Anne.　　　　　　　　　O, God's will! Much better
　　She ne'er had known pomp; though't be temporal,°
　　Yet, if that quarrel,° Fortune, do divorce
15　　It from the bearer, 'tis a sufferance panging°
　　As soul and body's severing.

Old Lady.　　　　　　　Alas, poor lady!
　　She's a stranger° now again.

Anne.　　　　　　　　　So much the more
　　Must pity drop upon her. Verily,
　　I swear, 'tis better to be lowly born

II.iii.1 **pinches** torments　4 **Pronounce** utter　6 **courses of the sun**
years　9 **this process** what has passed　10 **give her the avaunt**
order her to go　13 **temporal** worldly　14 **quarrel** quarreler (abstract for concrete)　15 **sufferance panging** suffering as agonizing
17 **stranger** foreigner

And range with humble livers° in content   20
Than to be perked up° in a glist'ring° grief
And wear a golden sorrow.

Old Lady.   Our content
Is our best having.°

Anne.   By my troth and maidenhead,
I would not be a queen.

Old Lady.   Beshrew me,° I would,
And venture maidenhead for't; and so would you,   25
For all this spice° of your hypocrisy.
You that have so fair parts° of woman on you,
Have too a woman's heart, which ever yet
Affected° eminence, wealth, sovereignty;
Which, to say sooth,° are blessings; and which gifts   30
(Saving your mincing)° the capacity
Of your soft cheveril° conscience would receive,
If you might please to stretch it.

Anne.   Nay, good troth.°

Old Lady. Yes, troth, and troth. You would not be
a queen?

Anne. No, not for all the riches under heaven.   35

Old Lady. 'Tis strange. A threepence bowed° would
hire me,
Old as I am, to queen° it. But, I pray you,
What think you of a duchess? Have you limbs
To bear that load of title?

Anne.   No, in truth.

Old Lady. Then you are weakly made. Pluck off° a
little;   40

20 **range with humble livers** rank with humble folk   21 **perked up**
decked out   21 **glist'ring** glittering   23 **having** possession   24 **Be-**
shrew me may evil befall me! (a mild imprecation)   26 **spice** dash,
sample   27 **parts** qualities (of mind and person)   29 **Affected**
aspired to   30 **say sooth** tell the truth   31 **Saving your mincing**
despite your coyness   32 **cheveril** kidskin   33 **troth** faith   36
bowed bent (and therefore worthless); with a possible quibble on
"bawd"   37 **queen** (with a pun on "quean" = bawd)   40 **Pluck off**
come down in rank

I would not be a young count° in your way,°
For more than blushing comes to. If your back
Cannot vouchsafe° this burden, 'tis too weak
Ever to get a boy.

Anne.   How you do talk!
45   I swear again, I would not be a queen
For all the world.

Old Lady.   In faith, for little England°
You'd venture an emballing.° I myself
Would for Caernarvonshire,° although there 'longed
No more to th' crown but that. Lo, who comes
    here?

Enter Lord Chamberlain.

Chamberlain. Good morrow, ladies. What were't worth
50   to know
The secret of your conference?°

Anne.   My good lord,
Not your demand; it values not° your asking.
Our mistress' sorrows we were pitying.

Chamberlain. It was a gentle business, and becoming
55   The action of good women. There is hope
All will be well.

Anne.   Now, I pray God, amen!

Chamberlain. You bear a gentle mind, and heav'nly
        blessings
Follow such creatures. That you may, fair lady,
Perceive I speak sincerely, and high note's
60   Ta'en of your many virtues, the King's Majesty
Commends his good opinion of you,° and

---

41 **count** (with a bawdy double meaning)   41 **way** (1) path (2) vir-
ginal condition   43 **vouchsafe** deign to accept   46 **little England**
(perhaps with a reference to Pembrokeshire, called "little England
beyond Wales"; word follows [line 63] of Anne's promotion to
Marchioness—historically, to Marquess—of Pembroke)   47 **emballing** investment with the ball as emblem of sovereignty (with a bawdy
pun)   48 **Caernarvonshire** a poor Welsh county   51 **conference**
conversation   52 **values not** is not worth   61 **Commends his good
opinion of you** presents his compliments

Does purpose honor to you no less flowing°
Than Marchioness of Pembroke; to which title
A thousand pound a year, annual support,
Out of his grace he adds.

Anne.   I do not know   65
What kind° of my obedience I should tender.
More than my all is nothing; nor my prayers
Are not° words duly hallowed, nor my wishes
More worth than empty vanities. Yet prayers and
    wishes
Are all I can return. Beseech your lordship,   70
Vouchsafe° to speak my thanks and my obedience,
As from a blushing handmaid, to his Highness,
Whose health and royalty I pray for.

Chamberlain.   Lady,
I shall not fail t' approve the fair conceit°
The King hath of you. [*Aside*] I have perused her
    well.   75
Beauty and honor in her are so mingled
That they have caught the King; and who knows
    yet
But from this lady may proceed a gem
To lighten all this isle?—I'll to the King,
And say I spoke with you.

Anne.   My honored lord.   80
                    Exit Lord Chamberlain.

Old Lady. Why, this it is:° see, see!
I have been begging sixteen years in court,
Am yet a courtier beggarly,° nor could
Come pat betwixt too early and too late
For any suit of pounds;° and you (O fate!)   85
A very fresh fish here—fie, fie, fie upon
This compelled° fortune!—have your mouth filled up
Before you open it.

62 **flowing** abundant   66 **kind** expression   67–68 **nor . . . not** (the
double negative lends emphasis)   71 **Vouchsafe** be good enough
74 **approve the fair conceit** confirm the good opinion   81 **this it is**
so it goes   83 **beggarly** (1) poor (2) begging   85 **suit of pounds**
i.e., petition for money   87 **compelled** i.e., forced upon her

Anne.   This is strange to me.

Old Lady. How tastes it? Is it bitter? Forty pence, no.
90 There was a lady once ('tis an old story)
  That would not be a queen, that would she not,
  For all the mud in Egypt.° Have you heard it?

Anne. Come, you are pleasant.

Old Lady.   With your theme, I could
  O'ermount° the lark. The Marchioness of Pem-
  broke?
95 A thousand pounds a year for pure respect?°
  No other obligation? By my life,
  That promises moe° thousands: honor's train
  Is longer than his foreskirt. By this time
  I know your back will bear a duchess. Say,
  Are you not stronger than you were?

100 *Anne.*   Good lady,
  Make yourself mirth with your particular fancy,
  And leave me out on't. Would I had no being,
  If this salute my blood° a jot. It faints me°
  To think what follows.
105 The Queen is comfortless, and we forgetful
  In our long absence. Pray, do not deliver°
  What here y'have heard to her.

Old Lady.   What do you think me?——
           Exeunt.

---

92 **mud in Egypt** riches of Egypt (the mud being the source of its fertility) 94 **O'ermount** fly higher than 95 **for pure respect** simply out of esteem 97 **moe** more 103 **salute my blood** exhilarates me 103 **faints me** makes me faint 106 **deliver** report

Scene IV. [*A hall in Blackfriars.*]

*Trumpets, sennet,° and cornets. Enter two Vergers,
with short silver wands; next them, two Scribes, in the
habit of doctors;° after them, the [Arch]bishop of
Canterbury alone; after him, the Bishops of Lincoln,
Ely, Rochester, and Saint Asaph. Next them, with
some small distance, follows a Gentleman bearing the
purse, with the Great Seal, and a cardinal's hat; then
two Priests, bearing each a silver cross; then a Gentleman Usher bareheaded, accompanied with a Sergeant
at Arms bearing a silver mace; then two Gentlemen
bearing two great silver pillars;° after them, side by
side, the two Cardinals; two Noblemen with the sword
and mace. The King takes place° under the cloth of
state;° the two Cardinals sit under him as judges. The
Queen takes place some distance from the King. The
Bishops place themselves on each side the court, in
manner of a consistory;° below them, the Scribes. The
Lords sit next the Bishops. The rest of the Attendants
stand in convenient order about the stage.*

Wolsey. Whilst our commission from Rome is read,
  Let silence be commanded.

King.   What's the need?
  It hath already publicly been read,
  And on all sides th' authority allowed.
  You may then spare that time.

Wolsey.   Be't so. Proceed.   5

Scribe. Say "Henry King of England, come into the
  court."

II.iv.s.d. **sennet** trumpet fanfare   **habit of doctors** i.e., capped and
gowned as doctors of law   **two great silver pillars** Wolsey's insignia   **takes place** takes his seat   **cloth of state** canopy   **consistory** College of Cardinals

Crier. Henry King of England, etc.

King. Here.

10 *Scribe.* Say "Katherine Queen of England, come into
the court."

Crier. Katherine Queen of England, etc.

> *The Queen makes no answer, rises out of her chair,
> goes about the court, comes to the King,
> and kneels at his feet; then speaks.*

Queen Katherine. Sir, I desire you do me right and
justice,
And to bestow your pity on me; for
15 I am a most poor woman and a stranger,
Born out of your dominions; having here
No judge indifferent,° nor no more assurance
Of equal friendship and proceeding.° Alas, sir,
In what have I offended you? What cause
20 Hath my behavior given to your displeasure
That thus you should proceed to put me off°
And take your good grace° from me? Heaven
witness,
I have been to you a true and humble wife,
At all times to your will conformable,
25 Ever in fear to kindle your dislike,
Yea, subject to your countenance, glad or sorry
As I saw it inclined. When was the hour
I ever contradicted your desire,
Or made it not mine too? Or which of your friends
30 Have I not strove to love, although I knew
He were mine enemy? What friend of mine
That had to him derived° your anger did I
Continue in my liking? Nay, gave° notice
He was from thence discharged? Sir, call to mind
35 That I have been your wife in this obedience
Upward of twenty years, and have been blessed

---

17 indifferent unbiased **18 equal friendship and proceeding** impartial friendship and proceedings **21 put me off** discard me 22
grace (1) self (2) favor **32 derived** incurred **33 gave** i.e. gave not

With many children by you. If, in the course
And process of this time, you can report,
And prove it too, against mine honor aught,
My bond to wedlock or my love and duty,
Against° your sacred person, in God's name,   40
Turn me away, and let the foul'st contempt
Shut door upon me, and so give me up
To the sharp'st kind of justice. Please you, sir,
The King, your father, was reputed for
A prince most prudent, of an excellent   45
And unmatched wit° and judgment. Ferdinand,
My father, King of Spain, was reckoned one
The wisest° prince that there had reigned by many
A year before. It is not to be questioned   50
That they had gathered a wise council to them
Of every realm, that did debate this business,
Who deemed our marriage lawful. Wherefore I
     humbly
Beseech you, sir, to spare me, till I may
Be by my friends in Spain advised, whose counsel   55
I will implore. If not, i' th' name of God,
Your pleasure be fulfilled!

Wolsey.   You have here, lady,
And of your choice, these reverend fathers, men
Of singular integrity and learning,
Yea, the elect o' th' land, who are assembled   60
To plead your cause. It shall be therefore bootless°
That longer you desire the court,° as well
For your own quiet,° as to rectify
What is unsettled in the King.

Campeius.   His Grace
Hath spoken well and justly. Therefore, madam,   65
It's fit this royal session do proceed,
And that without delay their arguments
Be now produced and heard.

41 **Against** (1) i.e., or aught against (?) (2) toward (?) 47 **wit**
intelligence 48–49 **one/The wisest** the very wisest 61 **bootless**
profitless 62 **longer you desire the court** longer you draw out
the business of the court (by pleading for a postponement) 63
quiet i.e., of mind

Queen Katherine.   Lord Cardinal,
To you I speak.

Wolsey.   Your pleasure, madam?

Queen Katherine.   Sir,
70 I am about to weep; but, thinking that
We are a queen, or long have dreamed so, certain°
The daughter of a king, my drops of tears
I'll turn to sparks of fire.

Wolsey.   Be patient yet.

Queen Katherine. I will, when you are humble; nay,
    before,
75 Or God will punish me. I do believe
(Induced by potent circumstances)° that
You are mine enemy, and make my challenge°
You shall not be my judge; for it is you
Have blown this coal° betwixt my lord and me—
80 Which God's dew quench! Therefore I say again,
I utterly abhor,° yea, from my soul
Refuse you for my judge, whom, yet once more,
I hold my most malicious foe, and think not
At all a friend to truth.

Wolsey.   I do profess
85 You speak not like yourself, who ever yet
Have stood to° charity and displayed th' effects
Of disposition gentle and of wisdom
O'ertopping woman's pow'r. Madam, you do me
    wrong:
I have no spleen° against you, nor injustice
90 For you or any. How far I have proceeded,
Or how far further shall, is warranted
By a commission from the consistory,
Yea, the whole consistory of Rome. You charge me
That I have blown this coal. I do deny it.

---

71 **certain** certainly   76 **Induced by potent circumstances** persuaded
by strong reasons   77 **challenge** objection (legal term)   79 **blown
this coal** stirred up this strife (proverbial)   81 **abhor** protest against
(legal term)   86 **stood to** supported   89 **spleen** malice

The King is present. If it be known to him   95
That I gainsay my deed,° how may he wound,
And worthily, my falsehood—yea, as much
As you have done my truth. If he know
That I am free of your report,° he knows
I am not of your wrong.° Therefore in him   100
It lies to cure me, and the cure is to
Remove these thoughts from you; the which before
His Highness shall speak in,° I do beseech
You, gracious madam, to unthink your speaking
And to say so no more.

Queen Katherine.   My lord, my lord,   105
I am a simple woman, much too weak
T' oppose your cunning. Y'are meek and
    humble-mouthed.
You sign your place and calling, in full seeming,
With meekness and humility,° but your heart
Is crammed with arrogancy, spleen, and pride.   110
You have by fortune and his Highness' favors
Gone slightly° o'er low steps, and now are mounted
Where pow'rs° are your retainers, and your words
(Domestics to you) serve your will as't please
Yourself pronounce their office.° I must tell you,   115
You tender° more your person's honor than
Your high profession spiritual; that again
I do refuse you for my judge, and here,
Before you all, appeal unto the Pope,
To bring my whole cause 'fore his Holiness,   120
And to be judged by him.
          She curtsies to the King, and offers to depart.

Campeius.   The Queen is obstinate,
Stubborn° to justice, apt to accuse it,° and

---

96 **gainsay my deed** now deny what I have done   99 **free of your report** innocent of your charges   100 **I am not of your wrong** i.e., I have been wronged by you   103 **in** regarding   108–09 **You sign . . . humility** to all outward appearances you set a stamp of meekness and humility on your high spiritual office   112 **slightly** easily   113 **pow'rs** those in power   113–15 **your words . . . office** i.e., your words are your servants, and you need only speak in order for your will to be done   116 **tender** value   122 **Stubborn** unpliant   122 **apt to accuse it** prone to call it in question

Disdainful to be tried by't. 'Tis not well.
She's going away.

125 *King.* Call her again.

Crier. Katherine Queen of England, come into the
    court.

Gentleman Usher. Madam, you are called back.

Queen Katherine. What need you note it? Pray you
    keep your way;°
When you are called, return. Now the Lord help!
130 They vex me past my patience. Pray you, pass on.
I will not tarry; no, nor ever more
Upon this business my appearance make
In any of their courts.

                Exit Queen, and her Attendants.

King.   Go thy ways, Kate.
That man i' th' world who shall report he has
135 A better wife, let him in naught be trusted,
For speaking false in that. Thou art, alone°—
If thy rare qualities, sweet gentleness,
Thy meekness saint-like, wife-like government,°
Obeying in commanding,° and thy parts
140 Sovereign and pious else, could speak thee out°—
The queen of earthly queens. She's noble born,
And like her true nobility she has
Carried herself towards me.

Wolsey.   Most gracious sir,
In humblest manner I require° your Highness,
145 That it shall please you to declare in hearing
Of all these ears—for where I am robbed and
    bound,
There must I be unloosed, although not there
At once and fully satisfied—whether ever I
Did broach this business to your Highness, or

---

128 **keep your way** keep going 136 **alone** without rival 138 **government** self-control 139 **Obeying in commanding** self-restrained
when giving orders 139–40 **thy parts . . . out** your other excellent
and pious qualities could describe you fully 144 **require** beg

Laid any scruple in your way which might   150
Induce you to the question on't? Or ever
Have to you, but with thanks to God for such
A royal lady, spake one the least° word that might
Be to the prejudice of her present state,
Or touch° of her good person?

King.   My Lord Cardinal,   155
I do excuse you; yea, upon mine honor,
I free you from't. You are not to be taught°
That you have many enemies that know not
Why they are so, but, like to village curs,
Bark when their fellows do. By some of these   160
The Queen is put in anger. Y'are excused.
But will you be more justified? You ever
Have wished the sleeping of this business, never
    desired
It to be stirred, but oft have hind'red, oft,
The passages° made toward it. On my honor   165
I speak° my good Lord Cardinal to this point,
And thus far clear him. Now, what moved me to't,
I will be bold with time and your attention.
Then mark th' inducement. Thus it came; give heed
    to't:
My conscience first received a tenderness,   170
Scruple, and prick, on certain speeches uttered
By th' Bishop of Bayonne, then French ambassador,
Who had been hither sent on the debating
A marriage 'twixt the Duke of Orleans and
Our daughter Mary. I' th' progress of this business, 175
Ere a determinate resolution,° he
(I mean the bishop) did require a respite,
Wherein he might the King his lord advertise°
Whether our daughter were legitimate,
Respecting this our marriage with the dowager,   180
Sometimes° our brother's wife. This respite shook

153 **one the least** a single   155 **touch** sullying   157 **You are not to be taught** you do not have to be told   165 **passages** proceedings   166 **speak** bear witness for   176 **determinate resolution** final decision   178 **advertise** inform (accent on second syllable)   181 **Sometimes** formerly

The bosom of my conscience, entered me,
Yea, with a spitting° power, and made to tremble
The region of my breast; which forced such way
185 That many mazed considerings° did throng,
And pressed in with this caution. First, methought
I stood not in the smile of heaven, who had
Commanded nature that my lady's womb,
If it conceived a male child by me, should
190 Do no more offices of life to't than
The grave does to th' dead; for her male issue
Or° died where they were made, or shortly after
This world had aired them. Hence I took a thought
This was a judgment on me, that my kingdom,
195 Well worthy the best heir o' th' world, should not
Be gladded in't by me. Then follows that
I weighed the danger which my realms stood in
By this my issue's fail,° and that gave to me
Many a groaning throe. Thus hulling° in
200 The wild sea of my conscience, I did steer
Toward this remedy whereupon we are
Now present here together. That's to say,
I meant to rectify° my conscience, which
I then did feel full sick, and yet° not well,
205 By all the reverend fathers of the land
And doctors learned. First I began in private
With you, my Lord of Lincoln. You remember
How under my oppression° I did reek,°
When I first moved° you.

Lincoln.   Very well, my liege.

210 *King.* I have spoke long. Be pleased yourself to say
How far you satisfied me.

Lincoln.   So please your Highness,
The question did at first so stagger me,

---

183 **spitting** as though impaled on a spit, transfixing 185 **mazed considerings** perplexed thoughts 192 **Or** either 198 **issue's fail** i.e., failure to have a son 199 **hulling** drifting with sail furled 203 **rectify** set right (cf. line 63) 204 **yet** now still 208 **oppression** heavy burden 208 **reek** sweat (literally smoke with heat) 209 **moved** proposed the matter

Bearing a state of mighty moment in't
And consequence of dread, that I committed
The daring'st counsel which I had to doubt,°   *215*
And did entreat your Highness to this course
Which you are running here.

King.   I then moved you,
My Lord of Canterbury, and got your leave
To make this present summons.° Unsolicited
I left no reverend person in this court,   *220*
But by particular consent proceeded
Under your hands and seals.° Therefore, go on;
For no dislike i' th' world against the person
Of the good Queen, but the sharp thorny points
Of my allegèd° reasons, drives this forward.   *225*
Prove but our marriage lawful, by my life
And kingly dignity, we are contented
To wear our mortal state to come with her,
Katherine our queen, before the primest° creature
That's paragoned° o' th' world.

Campeius.   So please your Highness,   *230*
The Queen being absent, 'tis a needful fitness
That we adjourn this court till further° day.
Meanwhile must be an earnest motion°
Made to the Queen to call back her appeal
She intends unto his Holiness.

King. [*Aside*]   I may perceive   *235*
These cardinals trifle with me. I abhor
This dilatory sloth and tricks of Rome.
My learned and well-belovèd servant, Cranmer,
Prithee return; with thy approach, I know,
My comfort comes along.—Break up the court;   *240*
I say, set on.

              Exeunt, in manner as they entered.

213–15 **Bearing . . . doubt** concerning so momentous a state of affairs, with consequences so dreadful to contemplate, that I did not
trust myself to give the boldest advice (i.e., that the marriage be
dissolved)   219 **summons** i.e., of the Queen   222 **Under your hands
and seals** with your signed and sealed consent   225 **allegèd** stated
229 **primest** foremost   230 **paragoned** held up as a paragon   232
further a more distant   233 **motion** appeal

ACT III

Scene I. [*London. The Queen's apartments.*]

Enter Queen and her Women, as at work.

Queen Katherine. Take thy lute, wench. My soul
  grows sad with troubles;
Sing and disperse 'em, if thou canst. Leave°
  working.

Song
Orpheus° with his lute made trees,
And the mountain tops that freeze,
   Bow themselves when he did sing.
To his music plants and flowers
Ever sprung, as sun and showers
   There had made a lasting spring.

Everything that heard him play,
Even the billows of the sea,
   Hung their heads, and then lay by.°
In sweet music is such art,
Killing care and grief of heart
   Fall asleep, or hearing die.

Enter a Gentleman.

15   *Queen Katherine.* How now?

III.i.2 **Leave** leave off   3 **Orpheus** (in mythology the music of his
lyre tamed wild beasts and entranced even inanimate nature)   11
lay by subsided

Gentleman. And't please your Grace, the two great cardinals
Wait in the presence.°

Queen Katherine.   Would they speak with me?

Gentleman. They willed me say so, madam.

Queen Katherine.   Pray their Graces
To come near. [*Exit Gentleman.*] What can be their business
With me, a poor weak woman, fall'n from favor?   20
I do not like their coming, now I think on't.
They should be good men, their affairs as righteous;°
But all hoods make not monks.

Enter the two Cardinals, Wolsey and Campeius.

Wolsey.   Peace to your Highness!

Queen Katherine. Your Graces find me here part of° a housewife.
I would be all, against the worst may happen.°   25
What are your pleasures with me, reverend lords?

Wolsey. May it please you, noble madam, to withdraw
Into your private chamber, we shall give you
The full cause of our coming.

Queen Katherine.   Speak it here;
There's nothing I have done yet, o' my conscience,   30
Deserves a corner. Would all other women
Could speak this with as free a soul as I do!
My lords, I care not (so much I am happy
Above a number) if my actions
Were tried by every tongue, every eye saw 'em,   35
Envy and base opinion° set against 'em,
I know my life so even.° If your business

---

17 presence presence chamber   **22 their affairs as righteous** i.e., their business should be as righteous as they themselves good   **24 part of** to some extent (because she is sewing)   **25 I would . . . happen** I would like to be a complete one, in preparation for the worst (i.e., in case I am divorced and left nothing else)   **36 Envy and base opinion** malice and unworthy gossip   **37 even** equable

Seek me out, and that way I am wife in,°
Out with it boldly: truth loves open dealing.

40 *Wolsey.* *Tanta est erga te mentis integritas, regina*
    serenissima°—

Queen Katherine. O, good my lord, no Latin;
    I am not such a truant since my coming,
    As not to know the language I have lived in.
    A strange tongue makes my cause more strange,
45   suspicious;°
    Pray speak in English. Here are some will thank
        you,
    If you speak truth, for their poor mistress' sake.
    Believe me, she has had much wrong. Lord Car-
        dinal,
    The willing'st° sin I ever yet committed
    May be absolved in English.

50 *Wolsey.*   Noble lady,
    I am sorry my integrity should breed
    (And service to his Majesty and you)
    So deep suspicion, where all° faith was meant.
    We come not by the way of accusation,
55 To taint that honor every good tongue blesses,
    Nor to betray you any way to sorrow—
    You have too much, good lady—but to know
    How you stand minded in the weighty difference
    Between the King and you, and to deliver,
60 Like free and honest men, our just opinions
    And comforts to your cause.

Campeius.   Most honored madam,
    My Lord of York, out of his noble nature,
    Zeal and obedience he still bore° your Grace,
    Forgetting, like a good man, your late censure
65 Both of his truth and him (which was too far)°

38 **Seek . . . wife in** concerns me, and my behavior as a wife   40–41
Tanta . . . serenissima so unprejudiced are we toward you, most
serene Queen   45 **strange, suspicious** foreign, and hence suspicious
49 **willing'st** most deliberate   53 **all** only   63 **still bore** has always borne   65 **far** extreme

Offers, as I do, in° a sign of peace,
His service and his counsel.

Queen Katherine. [*Aside*] To betray me.—
　My lords, I thank you both for your good wills.
　Ye speak like honest men; pray God ye prove so!
　But how to make ye suddenly° an answer,　　　　　　　*70*
　In such a point of weight, so near° mine honor,
　More near my life, I fear, with my weak wit,°
　And to such men of gravity and learning,
　In truth I know not. I was set° at work
　Among my maids, full little, God knows, looking　　　*75*
　Either for such men or such business.
　For her sake that I have been°—for I feel
　The last fit° of my greatness—good your Graces,
　Let me have time and counsel for my cause.
　Alas, I am a woman friendless, hopeless!　　　　　　　*80*

Wolsey. Madam, you wrong the King's love with these
　　fears.
　Your hopes and friends are infinite.

Queen Katherine.　　　　　　　　　In England
　But little for my profit. Can you think, lords,
　That any Englishman dare give me counsel
　Or be a known friend, 'gainst his Highness' plea-
　　sure—　　　　　　　　　　　　　　　　　　　*85*
　Though he be grown so desperate to be honest°—
　And live a subject? Nay, forsooth, my friends,
　They that must weigh out° my afflictions,
　They that my trust must grow to, live not here.
　They are, as all my other comforts, far hence　　　　*90*
　In mine own country, lords.

Campeius.　　　　　　　　　　I would your Grace
　Would leave your griefs, and take my counsel.

Queen Katherine.　　　　　　　　　　How, sir?

66 **in** as　70 **suddenly** on the spur of the moment　71 **near** closely
affecting　72 **wit** intelligence　74 **set** seated　77 **For her sake that
I have been** for what I once was　78 **fit** seizure (as in an illness)
86 **so desperate to be honest** i.e., so reckless as to come out hon-
estly in my support　88 **weigh out** attach full weight to

Campeius. Put your main cause into the King's protection;

He's loving and most gracious. 'Twill be much

95   Both for your honor better and your cause,°

For if the trial of the law o'ertake ye,

You'll part away° disgraced.

Wolsey.   He tells you rightly.

Queen Katherine. Ye tell me what ye wish for both—
my ruin.

Is this your Christian counsel? Out upon ye!

100   Heaven is above all yet; there sits a judge

That no king can corrupt.

Campeius.   Your rage mistakes us.

Queen Katherine. The more shame for ye. Holy men
I thought ye,

Upon my soul, two reverend cardinal virtues;°

But cardinal sins° and hollow hearts I fear ye.

Mend 'em, for shame, my lords. Is this your comfort?

105   The cordial that ye bring a wretched lady,

A woman lost among ye, laughed at, scorned?

I will not wish ye half my miseries:

I have more charity. But say I warned ye.

Take heed, for heaven's sake, take heed, lest at
once°

110   The burden of my sorrows fall upon ye.

Wolsey. Madam, this is a mere distraction.°

You turn the good we offer into envy.°

Queen Katherine. Ye turn me into nothing. Woe upon
ye,

115   And all such false professors!° Would you have me

---

95 **Both . . . cause** better for both your honor and your cause   97 **part away** depart   103 **cardinal virtues** the essential virtues (comprising fortitude, justice, prudence, and temperance); with a pun on the visitors' station   104 **cardinal sins** (alluding to the seven deadly sins; with pun on "carnal," the Elizabethan pronunciation of "cardinal")   110 **at once** all at once   112 **mere distraction** sheer madness   113 **envy** malice   115 **professors** i.e., of Christianity

(If you have any justice, any pity,
If ye be anything but churchmen's habits)°
Put my sick cause into his hands that hates me?
Alas, has banished me his bed already;
His love, too long ago! I am old,° my lords,   *120*
And all the fellowship I hold now with him
Is only my obedience. What can happen
To me above this wretchedness? All your studies
Make me a curse like this!°

Campeius.   Your fears are worse.°

Queen Katherine. Have I lived thus long (let me
          speak° myself,   *125*
Since virtue finds no friends) a wife, a true one?
A woman, I dare say without vainglory,
Never yet branded with suspicion?
Have I with all my full affections
Still met the King? Loved him next heaven? Obeyed
          him?   *130*
Been, out of fondness, superstitious to him?°
Almost forgot my prayers to content him?
And am I thus rewarded? 'Tis not well, lords.
Bring me a constant woman° to her husband,
One that ne'er dreamed a joy beyond his pleasure,° *135*
And to that woman, when she has done most,
Yet will I add an honor: a great patience.

Wolsey. Madam, you wander from the good we aim at.

Queen Katherine. My lord, I dare not make myself so
          guilty
To give up willingly that noble title   *140*
Your master wed me to. Nothing but death
Shall e'er divorce my dignities.

Wolsey.   Pray hear me.

---

117 habits garb   **120 old** (she was forty-three)   **123-24 All . . .
this** i.e., let all your learned efforts make my life any more wretched
than it already is   **124 worse** i.e., than your actual situation   **125
speak** describe   **131 superstitious to him** his idolator   **134 constant
woman** woman faithful   **135 pleasure** (1) enjoyment (2) wishes

Queen Katherine. Would I had never trod this English
    earth,
    Or felt the flatteries that grow upon it!
    Ye have angels' faces, but heaven knows your
145   hearts.°
    What will become of me now, wretched lady!
    I am the most unhappy woman living.
    Alas, poor wenches, where are now your fortunes?
    Shipwracked upon a kingdom, where no pity,
150   No friends, no hope; no kindred weep for me;
    Almost no grave allowed me. Like the lily,
    That once was mistress of the field, and flourished,
    I'll hang my head and perish.

Wolsey.   If your Grace
    Could but be brought to know our ends are
    honest,°
    You'd feel more comfort. Why should we, good
155   lady,
    Upon what cause, wrong you? Alas, our places,
    The way of our profession is against it.
    We are to cure such sorrows, not to sow 'em.
    For goodness' sake, consider what you do;
160   How you may hurt yourself, aye, utterly
    Grow° from the King's acquaintance, by this car-
    riage.°
    The hearts of princes kiss obedience,
    So much they love it; but to stubborn spirits
    They swell, and grow as terrible as storms.
165   I know you have a gentle, noble temper,
    A soul as even as a calm. Pray think us
    Those we profess, peacemakers, friends, and ser-
    vants.

Campeius. Madam, you'll find it so. You wrong your
    virtues
    With these weak women's fears. A noble spirit,
170   As yours was put into you, ever casts

---

145 **Ye have . . . hearts** (alluding to the proverbial "Fair face, foul
heart")   154 **ends are honest** intentions are honorable   161 **Grow**
be estranged   161 **carriage** conduct

Such doubts, as false coin, from it. The King loves
    you;
Beware you lose it not. For us, if you please
To trust us in your business, we are ready
To use our utmost studies° in your service.

Queen Katherine. Do what ye will, my lords; and pray
    forgive me.   *175*
If I have used myself° unmannerly,
You know I am a woman, lacking wit
To make a seemly answer to such persons.
Pray do my service° to his Majesty.
He has my heart yet, and shall have my prayers   *180*
While I shall have my life. Come, reverend fathers,
Bestow your counsels on me. She now begs
That little thought, when she set footing° here,
She should have bought her dignities so dear.
                                        Exeunt.

Scene II. [*Antechamber to the King's apartment.*]

    *Enter the Duke of Norfolk, Duke of Suffolk,
        Lord Surrey, and Lord Chamberlain.*

Norfolk. If you will now unite in your complaints
And force them with a constancy,° the Cardinal
Cannot stand under them. If you omit
The offer of this time,° I cannot promise
But that you shall sustain moe new disgraces,   *5*
With these you bear already.

Surrey.   I am joyful
To meet the least occasion that may give me

---

174 **studies** endeavors   176 **used myself** behaved   179 **do my service**
offer my respects   183 **footing** foot   III.ii.2 **force them with a
constancy** urge them with determination   3-4 **omit . . . time** neglect
this opportunity

Remembrance of my father-in-law, the Duke,°
To be revenged on him.

Suffolk.   Which of the peers
10 Have uncontemned° gone by him, or at least°
Strangely neglected? When did he regard
The stamp of nobleness in any person
Out of° himself?

Chamberlain.   My lords, you speak your plea-
    sures.°
What he deserves of you and me I know;
15 What we can do to him, though now the time
Gives way° to us, I much fear.° If you cannot
Bar his access to th' King, never attempt
Anything on him, for he hath a witchcraft
Over the King in's tongue.

Norfolk.   O, fear him not;
20 His spell in that is out.° The King hath found
Matter against him that forever mars
The honey of his language. No, he's settled,
Not to come off, in his displeasure.°

Surrey.   Sir,
I should be glad to hear such news as this
Once every hour.

25 *Norfolk.*   Believe it, this is true.
In the divorce his contrary proceedings°
Are all unfolded; wherein he appears
As I would wish mine enemy.

Surrey.   How came
His practices° to light?

8 **my father-in-law, the Duke** (Buckingham; see II.i.43–44)   10 **un-
contemned** undespised   10 **at least** i.e., have not at least been
13 **Out of** besides   13 **speak your pleasures** are free to say what
you care to   16 **way** scope   16 **fear** doubt   20 **His spell in that
is out** his influence that way is finished   22–23 **he's settled** . . .
displeasure i.e., he (Wolsey) is fixed, not to escape, in his (the
King's) displeasure (but "he" could possibly refer to the King, in
which case "come off" = desist)   26 **contrary proceedings** (1) proceedings contradicting their outward appearance (2) adverse proceedings   29 **practices** plots

Suffolk.   Most strangely.

Surrey.   O, how? How?

Suffolk. The Cardinal's letters to the Pope miscar-
   ried,   30
   And came to th' eye o' th' King; wherein was read
   How that the Cardinal did entreat his Holiness
   To stay the judgment o' th' divorce. For if
   It did take place, "I do" (quoth he), "perceive
   My king is tangled in affection to   35
   A creature° of the Queen's, Lady Anne Bullen."

Surrey. Has the King this?

Suffolk.   Believe it.

Surrey.   Will this work?

Chamberlain. The King in this perceives him how he
   coasts
   And hedges his own way.° But in this point
   All his tricks founder, and he brings his physic   40
   After his patient's death: the King already
   Hath married the fair lady.

Surrey.   Would he had!

Suffolk. May you be happy in your wish, my lord!
   For, I profess, you have it.

Surrey.   Now, all my joy
   Trace the conjunction!°

Suffolk.   My amen to't!

Norfolk.   All men's!   45

Suffolk. There's order given for her coronation.
   Marry, this is yet but young, and may be left
   To some ears unrecounted. But, my lords,
   She is a gallant creature and complete°

---

36 **creature** dependent   38–39 **coasts . . . way** moves circuitously
and stealthily (i.e., as by coasts and hedgerows) toward his own
goals   44–45 **all . . . conjunction** all the joy I can wish follow
the marriage   49 **complete** fully endowed

50   In mind and feature. I persuade me, from her
    Will fall some blessing to this land, which shall
    In it be memorized.°

Surrey.   But will the King
    Digest° this letter of the Cardinal's?
    The Lord forbid!

Norfolk.   Marry, amen!

Suffolk.   No, no.
55   There be moe wasps that buzz about his nose
    Will make this sting the sooner. Cardinal Campeius
    Is stol'n away to Rome; hath ta'en no leave;
    Has left the cause o' th' King unhandled, and
    Is posted° as the agent of our Cardinal
60   To second all his plot. I do assure you
    The King cried "Ha!" at this.

Chamberlain.   Now God incense him,
    And let him cry "Ha!" louder!

Norfolk.   But, my lord,
    When returns Cranmer?

Suffolk. He is returned in his opinions,° which
65   Have satisfied the King for his divorce,
    Together with all famous colleges
    Almost in Christendom. Shortly, I believe,
    His second marriage shall be published,° and
    Her coronation. Katherine no more
70   Shall be called Queen, but Princess Dowager
    And widow to Prince Arthur.

Norfolk.   This same Cranmer's
    A worthy fellow, and hath ta'en much pain
    In the King's business.

Suffolk.   He has, and we shall see him
    For it an archbishop.

---

52 memorized made memorable **53 Digest** stomach **59 posted** hastened **64 returned in his opinions** i.e., not in person, but in that the opinions have been received from him **68 published** proclaimed

Norfolk.   So I hear.

Suffolk.   'Tis so.

          Enter Wolsey and Cromwell.

     The Cardinal!

Norfolk. Observe, observe, he's moody.   75

Wolsey. The packet,° Cromwell,
     Gave't you the King?

Cromwell.   To his own hand, in's bedchamber.

Wolsey. Looked he o' th' inside of the paper?°

Cromwell.   Presently°
     He did unseal them, and the first he viewed,
     He did it with a serious mind; a heed   80
     Was in his countenance. You he bade
     Attend him here this morning.

Wolsey.   Is he ready
     To come abroad?

Cromwell.   I think by this he is.

Wolsey. Leave me awhile.

                         Exit Cromwell.

     [*Aside*] It shall be to the Duchess of Alençon,   85
     The French King's sister; he shall marry her.
     Anne Bullen? No. I'll no Anne Bullens for him;
     There's more in't than fair visage. Bullen?
     No, we'll no Bullens. Speedily I wish
     To hear from Rome. The Marchioness of Pem-
     broke!°   90

Norfolk. He's discontented.

Suffolk.   Maybe he hears the King
     Does whet his anger to° him.

---

76 packet parcel of state papers   **78 paper** wrapper   **78 Presently**
immediately   **90 Marchioness of Pembroke** (Anne did not in fact
receive the title until 1532, three years after the events of this
scene)   **92 to** against

Surrey.   Sharp enough,
Lord, for thy justice!

Wolsey. [*Aside*] The late queen's gentlewoman, a
knight's daughter,
95   To be her mistress' mistress? The Queen's queen?
This candle burns not clear. 'Tis I must snuff it;
Then out it goes.° What though I know her virtuous
And well deserving? Yet I know her for
A spleeny° Lutheran, and not wholesome to
100 Our cause that she should lie i' th' bosom of
Our hard-ruled° King. Again, there is sprung up
An heretic, an arch one, Cranmer, one
Hath° crawled into the favor of the King,
And is his oracle.

Norfolk.   He is vexed at something.

Enter King, reading of a schedule, [and Lovell].

Surrey. I would 'twere something that would fret the
105   string,°
The master-cord on's° heart.

Suffolk.   The King, the King!

King. What piles of wealth hath he accumulated
To his own portion! And what expense by th' hour
Seems to flow from him! How, i' th' name of thrift,
110 Does he rake this together? Now, my lords,
Saw you the Cardinal?°

Norfolk.   My lord, we have
Stood here observing him. Some strange commotion°
Is in his brain. He bites his lip, and starts;
Stops on a sudden, looks upon the ground,
115   Then lays his finger on his temple; straight

96–97 **This candle . . . goes** i.e., I will be called on to clear away
the impediments to this marriage, but instead will use the opportunity to quash it altogether ("snuff" = trim the wick)   99
spleeny (1) staunch (2) splenetic   101 **hard-ruled** difficult to manage   103 **Hath** that hath   105 **fret the string** gnaw through the
tendon   106 **on's** of his   111 **Saw you the Cardinal** (the King,
engrossed in the schedule [see s.d.], has not noticed Wolsey's
presence)   112 **commotion** turmoil, mutiny (see line 120)

Springs out into fast gait; then stops again,
Strikes his breast hard, and anon he casts
His eye against° the moon. In most strange postures
We have seen him set himself.

King.   It may well be
There is a mutiny in's mind. This morning   120
Papers of state he sent me to peruse,
As I required. And wot° you what I found
There, on my conscience, put unwittingly?
Forsooth, an inventory, thus importing:°
The several parcels° of his plate,° his treasure,   125
Rich stuffs,° and ornaments of household, which
I find at such proud rate° that it outspeaks
Possession of a subject.°

Norfolk.   It's heaven's will;
Some spirit put this paper in the packet
To bless your eye withal.

King.   If we did think   130
His contemplation were above the earth,
And fixed on spiritual object,° he should still
Dwell in his musings; but I am afraid
His thinkings are below the moon,° not worth
His serious considering.

> *King takes his seat; whispers Lovell, who*
> *goes to the Cardinal.*

Wolsey.   Heaven forgive me!   135
Ever God bless your Highness!

King.   Good my lord,
You are full of heavenly stuff,° and bear the in-
    ventory
Of your best graces in your mind; the which

---

118 **against** toward   122 **wot** know   124 **thus importing** conveying
this information   125 **several parcels** various particulars   125 **plate**
gold and silver household plate   126 **stuffs** cloths   127 **proud rate**
high value   127–28 **outspeaks . . . subject** describes more than a
subject should own   132 **spiritual object** a spiritual objective
134 **below the moon** worldly   137 **stuff** concerns (with a possible
quibble on the household stuff referred to in line 126)

You were now running o'er. You have scarce time
140 To steal from spiritual leisure° a brief span
To keep your earthly audit. Sure, in that
I deem you an ill husband,° and am glad
To have you therein my companion.

Wolsey.   Sir,
For holy offices I have a time; a time
145 To think upon the part of business which
I bear i' th' state; and Nature does require
Her times of preservation, which perforce
I, her frail son, amongst my brethren mortal,°
Must give my tendance° to.

King.   You have said well.

150 *Wolsey.* And ever may your Highness yoke together,
As I will lend you cause, my doing well
With my well saying!

King.   'Tis well said again,
And 'tis a kind of good deed to say well.
And yet words are no deeds. My father loved you;
155 He said he did, and with his deed did crown°
His word upon you. Since I had my office
I have kept you next my heart; have not alone
Employed you where high profits might come home,
But pared my present havings,° to bestow
My bounties upon you.

160 *Wolsey.* [*Aside*]   What should this mean?

Surrey. [*Aside*] The Lord increase this business!

King.   Have I not made you
The prime man of the state? I pray you tell me
If what I now pronounce you have found true;
And, if you may confess it, say withal,
165 If you are bound to us or no. What say you?

---

140 **spiritual leisure** religious occupations   142 **husband** manager
148 **amongst my brethren mortal** i.e., in my human (as distinguished
from divine) capacity   149 **tendance** attention   155 **crown** confirm
159 **havings** possessions

Wolsey. My sovereign, I confess your royal graces,
   Showered on me daily, have been more than could
   My studied purposes requite,° which went
   Beyond all man's endeavors. My endeavors
   Have ever come too short of my desires,   *170*
   Yet filed° with my abilities. Mine own ends
   Have been mine so that° evermore they pointed
   To th' good of your most sacred person and
   The profit of the state. For your great graces
   Heaped upon me, poor undeserver, I   *175*
   Can nothing render but allegiant° thanks,
   My prayers to heaven for you, my loyalty,
   Which ever has and ever shall be growing
   Till death, that winter, kill it.

King.   Fairly answered;
   A loyal and obedient subject is   *180*
   Therein illustrated. The honor of it
   Does pay the act of it, as, i' th' contrary,
   The foulness is the punishment.° I presume
   That, as my hand has opened bounty to you,
   My heart dropped love, my pow'r rained honor,
      more   *185*
   On you than any,° so your hand and heart,
   Your brain and every function of your power,
   Should, notwithstanding that° your bond of duty,
   As 'twere in love's particular,° be more
   To me, your friend, than any.

Wolsey.   I do profess   *190*
   That for your Highness' good I ever labored
   More° than mine own; that am, have,° and will
      be—
   Though all the world should crack their duty to you

167–68 **more . . . requite** more than I could with diligent endeavors
repay   171 **filed** kept pace   172 **so that** only to the extent that
176 **allegiant** loyal   181–83 **The honor . . . punishment** i.e., virtue
is its own reward, just as evil is its own punishment   186 **any** on
anyone   188 **notwithstanding that** over and above   189 **in love's
particular** out of personal affection   192 **More** (as in Buckingham's speech, I.i.184ff., the speaker's emotion overcomes the re-
straints of normal syntax in the rest of this speech, but the sense
is clear)   192 **have** have been

And throw it from their soul; though perils did
195 Abound as thick as thought could make 'em, and
Appear in forms more horrid—yet my duty,
As doth a rock against the chiding° flood,
Should the approach of this wild river break,°
And stand unshaken yours.

King.   'Tis nobly spoken.
200 Take notice, lords, he has a loyal breast,
For you have seen him open't. [*Giving him papers.*]
     Read o'er this;
And after, this; and then to breakfast with
What appetite you have.

          Exit King, frowning upon the Cardinal; the noble
               throng after him, smiling and whispering.

Wolsey.   What should this mean?
What sudden anger's this? How have I reaped it?
205 He parted frowning from me, as if ruin
Leaped from his eyes. So looks the chafèd° lion
Upon the daring huntsman that has galled° him,
Then makes him nothing.° I must read this paper;
I fear, the story of his anger. 'Tis so;
210 This paper has undone me. 'Tis th' account
Of all that world of wealth I have drawn together
For mine own ends; indeed, to gain the popedom,
And fee my friends in Rome. O negligence,
Fit for a fool to fall by! What cross° devil
215 Made me put this main° secret in the packet
I sent the King? Is there no way to cure this?
No new device to beat this from his brains?
I know 'twill stir him strongly; yet I know
A way, if it take right,° in spite of fortune
220 Will bring me off° again. What's this? "To th'
     Pope"?
The letter, as I live, with all the business
I writ to's Holiness. Nay then, farewell!

197 **chiding** tumultuous   198 **break** check   206 **chafèd** angry   207
galled wounded   208 **makes him nothing** annihilates him   214 **cross**
thwarting, perverse   215 **main** crucial   219 **take right** succeed
220 **bring me off** rescue me

I have touched the highest point of all my greatness,
And from that full meridian° of my glory
I haste now to my setting. I shall fall   225
Like a bright exhalation° in the evening,
And no man see me more.

*Enter to Wolsey the Dukes of Norfolk and Suffolk,
the Earl of Surrey, and the Lord Chamberlain.*

Norfolk. Hear the King's pleasure, Cardinal, who
    commands you
To render up the Great Seal° presently°
Into our hands, and to confine yourself   230
To Asher House, my Lord of Winchester's,°
Till you hear further from his Highness.

Wolsey.   Stay:
Where's your commission, lords? Words cannot carry
Authority so weighty.

Suffolk.   Who dare cross° 'em,
Bearing the King's will from his mouth expressly?   235

Wolsey. Till I find more than will or words to do it°—
I mean your malice—know, officious lords,
I dare, and must deny it. Now I feel
Of what coarse metal ye are molded—envy;
How eagerly ye follow my disgraces,   240
As if it fed ye! And how sleek and wanton°
Ye appear in everything may bring my ruin!
Follow your envious courses, men of malice;
You have Christian warrant° for 'em, and no doubt
In time will find their fit rewards. That seal   245
You ask with such a violence, the King,
Mine and your master, with his own hand gave me;
Bade me enjoy it, with the place and honors,

---

224 **meridian** (a star's highest point)   226 **exhalation** meteor   229
Great Seal (insignia of the Lord Chancellor's office; see I.i. 114s.d.n.)
229 **presently** at once   231 **Lord of Winchester's** (as Wolsey was
himself still Bishop of Winchester, we are perhaps meant to think
of his successor, Stephen Gardiner)   234 **cross** oppose   236 **do it**
(1) "render up the Great Seal" (line 229) (2) carry such great
authority   241 **wanton** unrestrained   244 **Christian warrant** justification by Christian principles (ironical)

During my life; and, to confirm his goodness,
250 Tied it by letters-patents.° Now, who'll take it?

Surrey. The King, that gave it.

Wolsey.   It must be himself, then.

Surrey. Thou art a proud traitor, priest.

Wolsey.   Proud lord, thou liest.
Within these forty hours Surrey durst better
Have burnt that tongue than said so.

Surrey.   Thy ambition,
255 Thou scarlet sin,° robbed this bewailing land
Of noble Buckingham, my father-in-law.
The heads of all thy brother cardinals,
With thee and all thy best parts° bound together,
Weighed° not a hair of his. Plague of your policy!
260 You sent me Deputy for Ireland;°
Far from his succor, from the King, from all
That might have mercy on the fault thou gav'st him,
Whilst your great goodness, out of holy pity,
Absolved him with an ax.

Wolsey.   This, and all else
265 This talking lord can lay upon my credit,°
I answer, is most false. The Duke by law
Found his deserts. How innocent I was
From any private malice in his end,
His noble jury and foul cause can witness.
270 If I loved many words, lord, I should tell you
You have as little honesty as honor,
That° in the way of loyalty and truth
Toward the King, my ever royal master,
Dare mate° a sounder man than Surrey can be,
And all that love his follies.

275 *Surrey.*   By my soul,

250 **Tied it by letters-patents** confirmed it by documents of formal conveyance   255 **scarlet sin** (referring to the color of his cassock, and also the traditional idea of scarlet sins, as in Isaiah 1:18)   258 **parts** qualities   259 **Weighed** equalled in weight   260 **Ireland** (three syllables)   265 **credit** reputation   272 **That** (the antecedent is "I," line 270)   274 **mate** match

Your long coat, priest, protects you; thou shouldst
    feel
My sword i' th' lifeblood of thee else. My lords,
Can ye endure to hear this arrogance?
And from this fellow? If we live thus tamely,
To be thus jaded° by a piece of scarlet,   *280*
Farewell nobility. Let his Grace go forward,
And dare us with his cap, like larks.°

Wolsey.   All goodness
Is poison to thy stomach.

Surrey.   Yes, that goodness
Of gleaning all the land's wealth into one,
Into your own hands, Card'nal, by extortion;   *285*
The goodness of your intercepted packets
You writ to th' Pope against the King. Your good-
    ness,
Since you provoke me, shall be most notorious.
My Lord of Norfolk,° as you are truly noble,
As you respect the common good, the state   *290*
Of our despised nobility, our issues,°
Who, if he live, will scarce be gentlemen,
Produce the grand sum of his sins, the articles°
Collected from his life. I'll startle you
Worse than the sacring bell,° when the brown
    wench   *295*
Lay kissing in your arms, Lord Cardinal.

Wolsey. How much, methinks, I could despise this
    man,
But that I am bound in charity against it!

Norfolk. Those articles, my lord, are in the King's
    hand;
But, thus much,° they are foul ones.

---

280 **jaded** intimidated   282 **dare us with his cap, like larks** i.e.,
dazzle us with his cardinal's hat, as larks were dazed and caught
by means of a mirror and piece of red cloth   289 **Lord of Norfolk**
(Norfolk was actually Surrey's father)   291 **issues** children   293
articles charges in an indictment   295 **sacring bell** the consecrating
bell rung at the elevation of the Host, the most solemn portion of
the Mass   300 **thus much** i.e., so much I can say

300 *Wolsey.*   So much fairer
And spotless shall mine innocence arise,
When the King knows my truth.

Surrey.   This cannot save you.
I thank my memory I yet remember
Some of these articles, and out they shall.
305 Now, if you can blush and cry "guilty," Cardinal,
You'll show a little honesty.

Wolsey.   Speak on, sir;
I dare your worst objections. If I blush,
It is to see a nobleman want° manners.

Surrey. I had rather want those than my head. Have
at you!°
310 First that, without the King's assent or knowledge,
You wrought to be a legate;° by which power
You maimed the jurisdiction of all bishops.

Norfolk. Then that in all you writ to Rome, or else
To foreign princes, *"Ego et Rex meus"*°
315 Was still inscribed; in which you brought the King
To be your servant.

Suffolk.   Then, that without the knowledge
Either of King or Council, when you went
Ambassador to the Emperor,° you made bold
To carry into Flanders the Great Seal.°

320 *Surrey.* Item, you sent a large commission
To Gregory de Cassado, to conclude,
Without the King's will or the state's allowance,
A league between his Highness and Ferrara.

---

308 **want** lack   309 **Have at you** here goes; cf. II.ii.85 (the six charges that follow are the most serious of the nine leveled against Wolsey; see appendix on sources)   311 **legate** i.e., the papal representative in England   314 **Ego et Rex meus** my King and I (the normal Latin word order, although Shakespeare followed the chroniclers in taking it to imply that Wolsey put himself before the King)   318 **Emperor** Charles V; see I.i.176–90   319 **To carry . . . Seal** (the Seal, and thus the Lord Chancellor, were not supposed to leave the country)

Suffolk. That out of mere° ambition you have caused
　　Your holy hat to be stamped on the King's coin.°　*325*

Surrey. Then that you have sent innumerable sub-
　　stance°
　　(By what means got, I leave to your own con-
　　science)
　　To furnish° Rome and to prepare the ways
　　You have for dignities, to the mere undoing
　　Of all the kingdom. Many more there are,　　*330*
　　Which, since they are of you and odious,
　　I will not taint my mouth with.

Chamberlain.　　　　　　　　O my lord,
　　Press not a falling man too far: 'tis virtue.°
　　His faults lie open to the laws; let them,
　　Not you, correct him. My heart weeps to see him　*335*
　　So little of his great self.

Surrey.　　　　　　　　I forgive him.

Suffolk. Lord Cardinal, the King's further pleasure
　　is—
　　Because all those things you have done of late,
　　By your power legative,° within this kingdom,
　　Fall into th' compass of a præmunire°—
　　That therefore such a writ be sued° against you:　*340*
　　To forfeit all your goods, lands, tenements,
　　Chattels, and whatsoever, and to be
　　Out of the King's protection. This is my charge.

Norfolk. And so we'll leave you to your meditations　*345*
　　How to live better. For your stubborn answer
　　About the giving back the Great Seal to us,
　　The King shall know it, and no doubt shall thank
　　you.
　　So fare you well, my little good Lord Cardinal.
　　　　　　　　　　　　　Exeunt all but Wolsey.

324 **mere** sheer　325 **Your holy ... coin** (a usurpation of royal pre-
rogative)　326 **innumerable substance** countless treasure　328 **furnish** supply　333 **virtue** i.e., to relent　339 **legative** as a papal
legate　340 **Fall ... præmunire** i.e., come within the penalties—
forfeiture of goods and outlawry—prescribed by the Statute of
Præmunire, which limited papal authority in England　341 **sued**
moved

350 *Wolsey.* So farewell to the little good you bear me.
     Farewell! A long farewell to all my greatness!
     This is the state of man: today he puts forth
     The tender leaves of hopes; tomorrow blossoms,
     And bears his blushing honors thick upon him.
355 The third day comes a frost, a killing frost,
     And, when he thinks, good easy° man, full surely
     His greatness is aripening, nips his root,
     And then he falls, as I do. I have ventured,
     Like little wanton° boys that swim on bladders,
360 This many summers in a sea of glory,
     But far beyond my depth. My high-blown pride
     At length broke under me and now has left me,
     Weary and old with service, to the mercy
     Of a rude° stream that must forever hide me.
365 Vain pomp and glory of this world, I hate ye.
     I feel my heart new opened. O, how wretched
     Is that poor man that hangs on princes' favors!
     There is betwixt that smile we would aspire to,
     That sweet aspect of princes, and their ruin,°
370 More pangs and fears than wars or women have.
     And when he falls, he falls like Lucifer,°
     Never to hope again.

            Enter Cromwell, standing amazed.

                          Why, how now, Cromwell?

Cromwell. I have no power to speak, sir.

Wolsey.   What, amazed
     At my misfortunes? Can thy spirit wonder
375 A great man should decline? Nay, and° you weep,
     I am fall'n indeed.

Cromwell.   How does your Grace?

Wolsey.   Why, well;
     Never so truly happy, my good Cromwell.

---

356 easy easygoing **359 wanton** playful **364 rude** turbulent **369
their ruin** the ruin they cause **371 he falls like Lucifer** (cf. Isaiah
14:12: "How art thou fallen from Heaven, O Lucifer, son of the
morning") **375 and** if

I know myself° now, and I feel within me
A peace above all earthly dignities,
A still and quiet conscience. The King has cured me,   380
I humbly thank his Grace; and from these shoulders,
These ruined pillars, out of pity, taken
A load would sink a navy—too much honor.
O, 'tis a burden, Cromwell, 'tis a burden
Too heavy for a man that hopes for heaven!   385

Cromwell. I am glad your Grace has made that right
    use of° it.

Wolsey. I hope I have. I am able now, methinks,
Out of a fortitude of soul I feel,
To endure more miseries and greater far
Than my weak-hearted enemies dare offer.   390
What news abroad?

Cromwell.   The heaviest and the worst
Is your displeasure° with the King.

Wolsey.   God bless him!

Cromwell. The next is, that Sir Thomas More is
    chosen
Lord Chancellor in your place.

Wolsey.   That's somewhat sudden.
But he's a learnèd man. May he continue   395
Long in his Highness' favor and do justice
For truth's sake and his conscience, that his bones,
When he has run his course and sleeps in blessings,
May have a tomb of orphans' tears wept on him!
What more?

Cromwell. That Cranmer is returned with welcome,   400
Installed Lord Archbishop of Canterbury.

Wolsey. That's news indeed.

Cromwell.   Last, that the Lady Anne,
Whom the King hath in secrecy long married,

---

378 **know myself** i.e., "recognize my limitations and my sins and
am able to transcend them" (Foakes)   386 **made that right use of**
derived that benefit from   392 **displeasure** loss of favor

This day was viewed in open as his queen,
405 Going to chapel; and the voice° is now
Only about her coronation.

Wolsey. There was the weight that pulled me down.
O Cromwell,
The King has gone beyond° me. All my glories
In that one woman I have lost forever.
410 No sun shall ever usher forth mine honors,
Or gild again the noble troops that waited
Upon my smiles. Go get thee from me, Cromwell;
I am a poor fall'n man, unworthy now
To be thy lord and master. Seek the King
415 (That sun I pray may never set!)—I have told him
What and how true thou art. He will advance thee;
Some little memory of me will stir him
(I know his noble nature) not to let
Thy hopeful service perish too. Good Cromwell,
420 Neglect him not; make use° now, and provide
For thine own future safety.

Cromwell.   O my lord,
Must I then leave you? Must I needs forgo°
So good, so noble, and so true a master?
Bear witness, all that have not hearts of iron,
425 With what a sorrow Cromwell leaves his lord.
The King shall have my service, but my prayers
Forever and forever shall be yours.

Wolsey. Cromwell, I did not think to shed a tear
In all my miseries, but thou hast forced me,
430 Out of thy honest truth,° to play the woman.
Let's dry our eyes—and thus far hear me, Cromwell,
And when I am forgotten, as I shall be,
And sleep in dull° cold marble where no mention
Of me more must be heard of, say I taught thee,
435 Say, Wolsey, that once trod the ways of glory,
And sounded all the depths and shoals of honor,

405 **voice** talk   408 **gone beyond** overreached   420 **make use** take
advantage   422 **forgo** forsake   430 **truth** faith   433 **dull** (1) inanimate (2) cheerless

Found thee a way, out of his wrack, to rise in:
A sure and safe one, though thy master missed it.
Mark but my fall and that that ruined me.
Cromwell, I charge thee, fling away ambition.   440
By that sin fell the angels. How can man then,
The image of his Maker, hope to win° by it?
Love thyself last; cherish those hearts that hate thee;
Corruption wins not more than honesty.
Still° in thy right hand carry gentle peace   445
To silence envious tongues. Be just, and fear not.
Let all the ends thou aim'st at be thy country's,
Thy God's, and truth's. Then if thou fall'st, O
     Cromwell,
Thou fall'st a blessed martyr.° Serve the King;
And prithee, lead me in.   450
There take an inventory of all I have
To the last penny; 'tis the King's. My robe,°
And my integrity to heaven, is all
I dare now call mine own. O Cromwell, Cromwell,
Had I but served my God with half the zeal   455
I served my King, he would not in mine age
Have left me naked to mine enemies.

Cromwell. Good sir, have patience.

Wolsey.   So I have. Farewell
The hopes of court! My hopes in heaven do dwell.
                                        Exeunt.

---

442 **win** profit   445 **Still** always   447–49 **Let . . . martyr** (after
becoming Earl of Essex and Lord Great Chamberlain, Cromwell
fell from favor and was beheaded in 1540)   452 **robe** i.e., cardinal's
habit

ACT IV

Scene I. [*A street in Westminster.*]

Enter two Gentlemen, meeting one another.

First Gentleman. Y'are well met once again.°

Second Gentleman.   So are you.

First Gentleman. You come to take your stand here, and behold
The Lady Anne pass from her coronation?

Second Gentleman. 'Tis all my business. At our last encounter
5   The Duke of Buckingham came from his trial.

First Gentleman. 'Tis very true. But that time offered sorrow;
This, general joy.

Second Gentleman.   'Tis well. The citizens,
I am sure, have shown at full their royal° minds—
As, let 'em have their rights, they are ever forward°—

IV.i.1 **again** (they met previously in II.i) 8 **royal** i.e., well disposed to the King 9 **let 'em have their rights, they are ever forward** to give them their due, they are always eager to do

In celebration of this day with shows,   10
Pageants, and sights of honor.

First Gentleman.   Never greater,
Nor, I'll assure you, better taken,° sir.

Second Gentleman. May I be bold to ask what that
     contains,
That paper in your hand?

First Gentleman.   Yes. 'Tis the list
Of those that claim their offices this day   15
By custom° of the coronation.
The Duke of Suffolk is the first, and claims
To be High Steward; next, the Duke of Norfolk,
He to be Earl Marshal. You may read the rest.

Second Gentleman. I thank you, sir; had I not known
     those customs,
I should have been beholding° to your paper.   20
But, I beseech you, what's become of Katherine,
The Princess Dowager? How goes her business?

First Gentleman. That I can tell you too. The Arch-
     bishop
Of Canterbury, accompanied with other   25
Learnèd and reverend fathers of his order,
Held a late° court at Dunstable, six miles off
From Ampthill, where the Princess lay; to which
She was often cited° by them, but appeared not.
And, to be short, for not appearance and   30
The King's late scruple, by the main assent°
Of all these learnèd men she was divorced,
And the late marriage made of none effect;°
Since which she was removed to Kimbolton,
Where she remains now sick.

Second Gentleman.   Alas, good lady!   35
                              [*Trumpets.*]

---

12 **taken** received   16 **By custom** i.e., in accordance with heredi-
tary privilege   21 **beholding** beholden   27 **late** recent   29 **cited**
summoned   31 **main assent** general agreement   33 **late marriage
made of none effect** former marriage annulled

The trumpets sound: stand close, the Queen is
  coming.

Hautboys.

THE ORDER OF THE CORONATION.

1. *A lively flourish° of trumpets.*
2. *Then two judges.*
3. *Lord Chancellor, with purse and mace before him.*
4. *Choristers, singing.*   *Music.°*
5. *Mayor of London, bearing the mace. Then Garter,°
   in his coat of arms, and on his head he wore a gilt
   copper crown.*
6. *Marquess Dorset, bearing a scepter of gold, on his
   head a demicoronal° of gold. With him, the Earl
   of Surrey, bearing the rod of silver with the dove,
   crowned with an earl's coronet. Collars of S's.°*
7. *Duke of Suffolk, in his robe of estate,° his coronet
   on his head, bearing a long white wand, as High
   Steward. With him, the Duke of Norfolk, with the
   rod of marshalship, a coronet on his head. Collars
   of S's.*
8. *A canopy borne by four of the Cinque-ports;°
   under it, the Queen in her robe, in her hair,°
   richly adorned with pearl, crowned. On each side
   her, the Bishops of London and Winchester.*
9. *The old Duchess of Norfolk, in a coronal of gold,
   wrought with flowers, bearing the Queen's train.*
10. *Certain Ladies or Countesses, with plain circlets
    of gold without flowers.*

*Exeunt, first passing over the stage in order and state,
and then a great flourish of trumpets. [As the procession passes, the two Gentlemen comment upon it.]*

36s.d. **flourish** fanfare   **Music** musicians   **Garter** i.e., Garter King-
at-Arms   **demicoronal** small coronet   **Collars of S's** gold chains
of office fashioned of S-shaped links   **estate** state   **four of the
Cinque-ports** i.e., four barons of the channel ports (the ports,
five in all, were Dover, Hastings, Hythe, Romney, and Sandwich)
in her hair with her hair hanging loosely (the custom for brides)

Second Gentleman. A royal train,° believe me. These
    I know.
  Who's that that bears the scepter?

First Gentleman.   Marquess Dorset;
  And that the Earl of Surrey, with the rod.

Second Gentleman. A bold brave gentleman. That
    should be   40
  The Duke of Suffolk?

First Gentleman.   'Tis the same: High Steward.

Second Gentleman. And that my Lord of Norfolk?

First Gentleman.   Yes.

Second Gentleman. [*Looking on the Queen*] Heaven
    bless thee!
  Thou hast the sweetest face I ever looked on.
  Sir, as I have a soul, she is an angel;
  Our King has all the Indies° in his arms,   45
  And more and richer, when he strains° that lady.
  I cannot blame his conscience.

First Gentleman.   They that bear
  The cloth of honor over her, are four barons
  Of the Cinque-ports.

Second Gentleman. Those men are happy, and so are
    all are near her.   50
  I take it, she that carries up the train
  Is that old noble lady, Duchess of Norfolk.

First Gentleman. It is, and all the rest are countesses.

Second Gentleman. Their coronets say so. These are
    stars indeed.

First Gentleman. And sometimes falling° ones.

Second Gentleman.   No more of that. 55

---

37 train retinue **45 all the Indies** i.e., the East and the West (the
Indies were celebrated for their riches) **46 strains** clasps **55 falling** (with a *double-entendre;* "falling" = surrendering chastity)

[*The last of the procession exits; trumpets sound.*]

Enter a third Gentleman.

First Gentleman. God save you, sir! Where have you
    been broiling?

Third Gentleman. Among the crowd i' th' abbey,
    where a finger
Could not be wedged in more: I am stifled
With the mere rankness° of their joy.

Second Gentleman.   You saw
    The ceremony?

Third Gentleman. That I did.

60 *First Gentleman.*   How was it?

Third Gentleman. Well worth the seeing.

Second Gentleman.   Good sir, speak° it to us.

Third Gentleman. As well as I am able. The rich
    stream
Of lords and ladies, having brought the Queen
To a prepared place in the choir, fell off°
65 A distance from her, while her Grace sat down
To rest awhile, some half an hour or so,
In a rich chair of state, opposing° freely
The beauty of her person to the people.
Believe me, sir, she is the goodliest woman
70 That ever lay by man; which when the people
Had the full view of, such a noise arose
As the shrouds° make at sea in a stiff tempest,
As loud and to as many tunes; hats, cloaks—
Doublets,° I think—flew up, and had their faces
75 Been loose, this day they had been lost. Such joy
I never saw before. Great-bellied° women

59 **mere rankness** sheer stink   61 **speak** describe   64 **off** back   67
opposing exposing   72 **shrouds** sail-ropes   74 **Doublets** men's close-
fitting garments, with or without sleeves   76 **Great-bellied** pregnant

That had not half a week to go, like rams°
In the old time of war, would shake the press,°
And make 'em reel before 'em. No man living
Could say "This is my wife" there, all were woven   80
So strangely in one piece.

Second Gentleman.   But what followed?

Third Gentleman. At length her Grace rose, and with
          modest paces
Came to the altar, where she kneeled and saintlike
Cast her fair eyes to heaven and prayed devoutly;
Then rose again and bowed her to the people;   85
When by the Archbishop of Canterbury
She had all the royal makings of° a queen,
As° holy oil, Edward Confessor's crown,
The rod, and bird of peace, and all such emblems
Laid nobly on her; which performed, the choir,   90
With all the choicest music° of the kingdom,
Together sung "Te Deum." So she parted,°
And with the same full state° paced back again
To York Place, where the feast is held.°

First Gentleman.   Sir,
You must no more call it York Place; that's past.   95
For, since the Cardinal fell, that title's lost:°
'Tis now the King's, and called Whitehall.

Third Gentleman.   I know it,
But 'tis so lately altered that the old name
Is fresh about me.

Second Gentleman. What two reverend bishops
Were those that went on each side of the Queen?   100

Third Gentleman. Stokesly and Gardiner; the one of
          Winchester,
Newly preferred from° the King's secretary,
The other, London.

77 rams battering rams   **78 press** crowd   **87 makings of** things that
go to make   **88 As** namely   **91 music** musicians   **92 parted** departed   **93 state** pomp   **94 To York . . . held** (it was in fact held
in Westminster Hall; the change permits the reference to Wolsey
which follows)   **96 lost** erased   **102 preferred from** promoted from
being

Second Gentleman.   He of Winchester
Is held no great good lover of the Archbishop's,
The virtuous Cranmer.

105 *Third Gentleman.*   All the land knows that;
However, yet there is no great breach. When it
     comes,
Cranmer will find a friend will° not shrink from
     him.

Second Gentleman. Who may that be, I pray you?

Third Gentleman.   Thomas Cromwell,
A man in much esteem with th' King, and truly
110 A worthy friend. The King has made him Master
O' th' Jewel House,
And one, already, of the Privy Council.

Second Gentleman. He will deserve more.

Third Gentleman.   Yes, without all doubt.
Come, gentlemen, ye shall go my way,
Which is to th' court, and there ye shall be my
115   guests;
Something° I can command. As I walk thither,
I'll tell ye more.

Both.   You may command us, sir.
                         Exeunt.

Scene II. [*Kimbolton.*]

*Enter Katherine, Dowager, sick; led between
Griffith, her Gentleman Usher, and
Patience, her woman.*

Griffith. How does your Grace?

Katherine.   O Griffith, sick to death.
My legs like loaden branches bow to th' earth,

107 **will** who will   116 **Something** to some extent

Willing to leave their burden. Reach a chair.
So—now, methinks, I feel a little ease.
Didst thou not tell me, Griffith, as thou led'st me,　　*5*
That the great child of honor, Cardinal Wolsey,
Was dead?°

Griffith.　　　　Yes, madam; but I think your Grace,
Out of the pain you suffered, gave no ear to't.

Katherine. Prithee, good Griffith, tell me how he
　　died.
If well, he stepped before me happily°　　　　　　*10*
For my example.

Griffith.　　　　　Well, the voice goes,° madam.
For after the stout Earl Northumberland
Arrested him at York, and brought him forward,
As a man sorely tainted,° to his answer,
He fell sick suddenly, and grew so ill　　　　　　*15*
He could not sit his mule.

Katherine.　　　　　Alas, poor man!

Griffith. At last, with easy roads,° he came to Leices-
　　ter,
Lodged in the abbey; where the reverend abbot,
With all his covent,° honorably received him;
To whom he gave these words: "O father abbot,　　*20*
An old man broken with the storms of state
Is come to lay his weary bones among ye;
Give him a little earth for charity."
So went to bed, where eagerly° his sickness
Pursued him still; and three nights after this,　　*25*
About the hour of eight, which he himself
Foretold should be his last, full of repentance,
Continual meditations, tears, and sorrows,
He gave his honors to the world again,
His blessèd part° to heaven, and slept in peace.　　*30*

IV.ii.7 **dead** (Wolsey died in 1530, Katherine in 1536)　10 **happily**
(1) appropriately (2) perhaps　11 **the voice goes** people say　14
sorely tainted severely disgraced　17 **roads** stages　19 **covent** convent (used of religious companies of either sex)　24 **eagerly** sharply
30 **blessèd part** soul

Katherine. So may he rest. His faults lie gently on
    him!
    Yet thus far, Griffith, give me leave to speak° him,
    And yet with charity. He was a man
    Of an unbounded stomach,° ever ranking
35   Himself with princes; one that by suggestion
    Tied° all the kingdom. Simony° was fair play;
    His own opinion was his law. I' th' presence°
    He would say untruths and be ever double°
    Both in his words and meaning. He was never,
40   But where he meant to ruin, pitiful.
    His promises were, as he then was, mighty,
    But his performance, as he is now, nothing.
    Of his own body he was ill,° and gave
    The clergy ill example.

Griffith.   Noble madam,
45   Men's evil manners live in brass; their virtues
    We write in water. May it please your Highness
    To hear me speak his good° now?

Katherine.   Yes, good Griffith;
    I were malicious else.

Griffith.   This Cardinal,
    Though from an humble stock, undoubtedly
50   Was fashioned to much honor from his cradle.
    He was a scholar, and a ripe and good one;
    Exceeding wise, fair-spoken, and persuading;
    Lofty and sour to them that loved him not,
    But to those men that sought him, sweet as summer.
55   And though he were unsatisfied in getting,°
    Which was a sin, yet in bestowing, madam,
    He was most princely: ever witness for him
    Those twins of learning that he raised in you,°

---

32 **speak** describe   34 **stomach** arrogance   35–36 **by suggestion/
Tied** by underhand dealing brought into bondage   36 **Simony** the
buying and selling of ecclesiastical preferment   37 **presence** presence chamber, i.e., before the King   38 **double** deceitful   43 **Of
his own body he was ill** i.e., he was depraved in his sexual conduct   47 **speak his good** describe his good qualities   55 **unsatisfied in getting** insatiably acquisitive   58 **raised in you** i.e., erected
in your cities

Ipswich and Oxford; one of which fell with him,
Unwilling to outlive the good° that did it;   60
The other,° though unfinished, yet so famous,
So excellent in art,° and still so rising,
That Christendom shall ever speak his virtue.
His overthrow heaped happiness upon him,
For then, and not till then, he felt himself,°   65
And found the blessedness of being little.
And, to add greater honors to his age
Than man could give him, he died fearing God.

Katherine. After my death I wish no other herald,
No other speaker of my living actions,°   70
To keep mine honor from corruption,
But such an honest chronicler as Griffith.
Whom° I most hated living, thou hast made me,
With thy religious truth and modesty,°
Now in his ashes honor. Peace be with him!   75
Patience, be near me still, and set me lower:
I have not long to trouble thee. Good Griffith,
Cause the musicians play me that sad note°
I named my knell, whilst I sit meditating
On that celestial harmony° I go to.   80

                    Sad and solemn music.

Griffith. She is asleep. Good wench, let's sit down
    quiet,
For fear we wake her. Softly, gentle Patience.

                    The Vision.

*Enter, solemnly tripping° one after another, six per-
sonages, clad in white robes, wearing on their heads
garlands of bays,° and golden vizards° on their faces;*

---

60 **good** goodness   61 **other** i.e., Christ Church, Oxford   62 **art**
learning   65 **felt himself** truly knew himself   70 **living actions**
actions during my life   73 **Whom** (object of "hated"; also of
"honor" in line 75)   74 **religious truth and modesty** strict truth and
moderation   78 **note** tune   80 **celestial harmony** (the heavenly
spheres in their revolutions were thought to produce a music accessible only to the liberated soul)   82s.d. **tripping** with light steps
bays bay leaves (symbolic of triumph)   **vizards** masks (probably
to indicate that they are spirits)

branches of bays or palm in their hands. They first
congee° unto her, then dance; and, at certain
changes,° the first two hold a spare garland over her
head; at which the other four make reverent curtsies.
Then the two that held the garland deliver the same to
the other next two, who observe the same order in
their changes, and holding the garland over her head;
which done, they deliver the same garland to the last
two, who likewise observe the same order; at which,
as it were by inspiration, she makes in her sleep signs
of rejoicing, and holdeth up her hands to heaven. And
so in their dancing vanish, carrying the garland with
them. The music continues.

Katherine. Spirits of peace, where are ye? Are ye all
          gone,
     And leave me here in wretchedness behind ye?

Griffith. Madam, we are here.

85 *Katherine.*   It is not you I call for.
     Saw ye none enter since I slept?

Griffith.   None, madam.

Katherine. No? Saw you not even now a blessèd troop
     Invite me to a banquet, whose bright faces
     Cast thousand beams upon me, like the sun?
90   They promised me eternal happiness,
     And brought me garlands, Griffith, which I feel
     I am not worthy yet to wear. I shall, assuredly.

Griffith. I am most joyful, madam, such good dreams
     Possess your fancy.

Katherine.   Bid the music leave;°
     They are harsh and heavy to me.   *Music ceases.*

95 *Patience.*   Do you note
     How much her Grace is altered on the sudden?
     How long her face is drawn? How pale she looks,
     And of an earthy cold? Mark her eyes.

congee bow ceremoniously   **changes** movements in the dance   94
music leave musicians stop

Griffith. She is going, wench. Pray, pray.

Patience.   Heaven comfort her!

> *Enter a Messenger.*

Messenger. And't like° your Grace—

Katherine.   You are a saucy fellow!   *100*
  Deserve we no more reverence?

Griffith.   You are to blame,
  Knowing she will not lose° her wonted greatness,
  To use so rude behavior. Go to, kneel.

Messenger. I humbly do entreat your Highness' par-
  don:
  My haste made me unmannerly. There is staying°   *105*
  A gentleman, sent from the King, to see you.

Katherine. Admit him entrance, Griffith; but this
  fellow
  Let me ne'er see again.   *Exit Messenger.*

> *Enter Lord Capucius.°*
>   If my sight fail not,
  You should be Lord Ambassador from the Em-
  peror,
  My royal nephew, and your name Capucius.   *110*

Capucius. Madam, the same. Your servant.

Katherine.   O, my lord,
  The times and titles now are altered strangely
  With me since first you knew me. But I pray you,
  What is your pleasure with me?

Capucius.   Noble lady,
  First, mine own service to your Grace; the next,   *115*
  The King's request that I would visit you,
  Who grieves much for your weakness, and by me

---

100 **And't like** if it please   102 **lose** give up   105 **staying** waiting
108s.d. **Exit . . . Capucius** (most editors have Griffith exit with the
messenger and re-enter with Capucius, but he need not leave the
stage in order to usher in the visitor)

Sends you his princely commendations,°
And heartily entreats you take good comfort.

Katherine. O my good lord, that comfort comes too
120   late;
'Tis like a pardon after execution.°
That gentle physic,° given in time, had cured me,
But now I am past all comforts here° but prayers.
How does his Highness?

Capucius.   Madam, in good health.

125 *Katherine.* So may he ever do, and ever flourish,
When I shall dwell with worms, and my poor name
Banished the kingdom! Patience, is that letter
I caused you write yet sent away?

Patience.   No, madam.
                    [*Giving it to Katherine.*]

Katherine. Sir, I most humbly pray you to deliver
This to my lord the King.

130 *Capucius.*   Most willing, madam.

Katherine. In which I have commended to his good-
            ness
The model° of our chaste loves, his young daugh-
            ter°—
The dews of heaven fall thick in blessings on her!—
Beseeching him to give her virtuous breeding°—
135 She is young, and of a noble modest nature;
I hope she will deserve well—and a little
To love her for her mother's sake that loved him
Heaven knows how dearly. My next poor petition
Is that his noble Grace would have some pity
140 Upon my wretched women that so long
Have followed both my fortunes° faithfully;
Of which there is not one, I dare avow

118 **commendations** greetings   121 **execution** ("-tion" two syllables)   122 **physic** healing art   123 **here** i.e., in this world   132
model image   132 **daughter** Mary, afterward Queen (1553–58)   134
breeding upbringing   141 **both my fortunes** i.e., my good fortune
and bad

(And now° I should not lie), but will deserve,
For virtue and true beauty of the soul,
For honesty and decent carriage,   145
A right good husband, let him be° a noble;
And, sure, those men are happy that shall have 'em.
The last is, for my men—they are the poorest,
But poverty could never draw 'em from me—
That they may have their wages duly paid 'em,   150
And something over to remember me by.
If heaven had pleased to have given me longer life
And able° means, we had not parted thus.
These are the whole contents; and, good my lord,
By that you love the dearest in this world,   155
As you wish Christian peace to souls departed,
Stand these poor people's friend, and urge the King
To do me this last right.

Capucius.   By heaven, I will,
Or let me lose the fashion° of a man!

Katherine. I thank you, honest lord. Remember me   160
In all humility unto his Highness.
Say his long trouble now is passing
Out of this world. Tell him in death I blessed him,
For so I will. Mine eyes grow dim. Farewell,
My lord. Griffith, farewell. Nay, Patience,   165
You must not leave me yet. I must to bed;
Call in more women. When I am dead, good wench,
Let me be used with honor. Strew me over
With maiden flowers,° that all the world may know
I was a chaste wife to my grave. Embalm me,   170
Then lay me forth. Although unqueened, yet like
A queen and daughter to a king, inter me.
I can° no more.   *Exeunt, leading Katherine.*

---

143 **now** i.e., at the point of death   146 **let him be** i.e., even   153
able sufficient   159 **fashion** form, nature   169 **maiden flowers** i.e.,
flowers appropriate to one who was chaste   173 **can** i.e., can do

ACT V

Scene I. [*London. A gallery in the palace.*]

*Enter Gardiner, Bishop of Winchester,
a Page with a torch before him,
met by Sir Thomas Lovell.*

Gardiner. It's one o'clock, boy, is't not?

Boy.   It hath struck.

Gardiner. These should be hours for necessities,
  Not for delights; times to repair our nature
  With comforting repose, and not for us
  To waste these times. Good hour of night, Sir
5   Thomas!
  Whither so late?

Lovell.   Came you from the King, my lord?

Gardiner. I did, Sir Thomas, and left him at primero°
  With the Duke of Suffolk.

Lovell.   I must to him too
  Before he go to bed. I'll take my leave.

Gardiner. Not yet, Sir Thomas Lovell. What's the
10   matter?
  It seems you are in haste; and if there be

V.i.7 **primero** a card game

142

No great offense belongs to't, give your friend
Some touch° of your late business. Affairs that walk
(As they say spirits do) at midnight have
In them a wilder nature than the business   *15*
That seeks dispatch by day.

Lovell.   My lord, I love you,
And durst commend a secret to your ear
Much weightier than this work. The Queen's in labor,
They say, in great extremity, and feared
She'll with the labor end.

Gardiner.   The fruit she goes with   *20*
I pray for heartily, that it may find
Good time,° and live; but for the stock,° Sir Thomas,
I wish it grubbed up now.

Lovell.   Methinks I could
Cry thee amen,° and yet my conscience says
She's a good creature and, sweet lady, does   *25*
Deserve our better wishes.

Gardiner.   But, sir, sir,
Hear me, Sir Thomas. Y'are a gentleman
Of mine own way;° I know you wise, religious;
And, let me tell you, it will ne'er be well—
'Twill not, Sir Thomas Lovell, take't of me—   *30*
Till Cranmer, Cromwell (her two hands)° and she
Sleep in their graves.

Lovell.   Now, sir, you speak of two
The most remarked° i' th' kingdom. As for Cromwell,
Beside that of the Jewel House, is made Master
O' th' Rolls,° and the King's secretary; further, sir,   *35*
Stands in the gap and trade° of moe preferments,

13 **touch** inkling   22 **Good time** i.e., a safe delivery   22 **stock**
trunk (of a tree), i.e., the Queen   24 **Cry thee amen** i.e., second
you   28 **way** i.e., religious persuasion (anti-Lutheran)   31 **hands**
supporters   33 **remarked** in the public eye   34–35 **Master/O' th'
Rolls** Keeper of the Records   36 **gap and trade** entrance and beaten
path

With which the time° will load him. Th' Archbishop
Is the King's hand and tongue, and who dare speak
One syllable against him?

Gardiner.   Yes, yes, Sir Thomas,
40   There are that dare, and I myself have ventured
To speak my mind of him. And indeed this day,
Sir, I may tell it you, I think I have
Insensed° the lords o' th' council that he is
(For, so I know he is, they know he is)°
45   A most arch heretic, a pestilence
That does infect the land; with which they moved°
Have broken with° the King, who hath so far
Given ear to our complaint, of his great grace
And princely care foreseeing those fell° mischiefs
50   Our reasons° laid before him, hath° commanded
Tomorrow morning to the council board
He be convented.° He's a rank weed, Sir Thomas,
And we must root him out. From your affairs
I hinder you too long. Good night, Sir Thomas.
                              Exit Gardiner and Page.

55   *Lovell.* Many good nights, my lord; I rest your servant.

                    Enter King and Suffolk.

King. Charles, I will play no more tonight.
My mind's not on't; you are too hard for me.

Suffolk. Sir, I did never win of you before.

King. But little, Charles,
60   Nor shall not, when my fancy's on my play.
Now, Lovell, from the Queen what is the news?

Lovell. I could not personally deliver to her
What you commanded me, but by her woman
I sent your message; who° returned her thanks

37 **time** i.e., the trend of the times   43 **Insensed** (1) informed (2)
stirred up ("insensed" = incensed)   44 **For . . . they know he is**
i.e., for if I know he is, then I can make them know   46 **moved**
angered   47 **broken with** broken the information to   49 **fell** ter-
rible   50 **reasons** account, explanation   50 **hath** i.e., that he has
52 **convented** summoned   64 **who** and who (i.e., the Queen)

In the great'st humbleness, and desired your Highness   65
Most heartily to pray for her.

King.   What say'st thou, ha?
To pray for her? What, is she crying out?

Lovell. So said her woman, and that her suff'rance°
   made
Almost each pang a death.

King.   Alas, good lady!

Suffolk. God safely quit° her of her burden, and   70
With gentle travail, to the gladding of
Your Highness with an heir!

King.   'Tis midnight, Charles;
Prithee, to bed, and in thy prayers remember
Th' estate° of my poor queen. Leave me alone,
For I must think of that which company   75
Would not be friendly to.°

Suffolk.   I wish your Highness
A quiet night, and my good mistress will
Remember in my prayers.

King.   Charles, good night. *Exit Suffolk.*

     Enter Sir Anthony Denny.

Well, sir, what follows?

Denny. Sir, I have brought my lord the Archbishop,   80
As you commanded me.

King.   Ha? Canterbury?

Denny. Aye, my good lord.

King.   'Tis true: where is he, Denny?

Denny. He attends your Highness' pleasure.

---

68 **suff'rance** suffering   70 **quit** release   74 **estate** condition   75–76
that which . . . friendly to i.e., matters for which company would
not be helpful

King.   Bring him to us.
                                    [*Exit Denny.*]

Lovell. [*Aside*] This is about that which the bishop°
        spake;
85   I am happily° come hither.

                Enter Cranmer and Denny.

King. Avoid° the gallery. (*Lovell seems to stay.*) Ha!
        I have said.° Be gone.
What!   *Exeunt Lovell and Denny.*

Cranmer. [*Aside*] I am fearful.° Wherefore frowns he
        thus?
        'Tis his aspect° of terror. All's not well.

King. How now, my lord? You do desire to know
        Wherefore I sent for you.

90   *Cranmer.* [*Kneeling*]   It is my duty
        T' attend your Highness' pleasure.

King.   Pray you, arise,
        My good and gracious Lord of Canterbury.
        Come, you and I must walk a turn together;
        I have news to tell you. Come, come, give me
            your hand.
95   Ah, my good lord, I grieve at what I speak,
        And am right sorry to repeat what follows.
        I have, and most unwillingly, of late
        Heard many grievous, I do say, my lord,
        Grievous complaints of you; which, being consid-
            ered,
100   Have moved° us and our council, that you shall
        This morning come before us; where I know
        You cannot with such freedom purge° yourself
        But that, till further trial in those charges
        Which will require your answer, you must take
105   Your patience to you and be well contented

---

84 **bishop** Gardiner   85 **happily** opportunely   86 **Avoid** leave   86
said spoken   87 **fearful** afraid   88 **aspect** expression (accent on
second syllable)   100 **moved** persuaded   102 **purge** i.e., of guilt

To make your house our Tow'r.° You a brother of
  us,°
It fits we thus proceed, or else no witness
Would come against you.

Cranmer. [*Kneeling*]   I humbly thank your Highness,
  And am right glad to catch this good occasion
  Most throughly° to be winnowèd, where my chaff   110
  And corn° shall fly asunder; for I know
  There's none stands under° more calumnious
    tongues
  Than I myself, poor man.

King.   Stand up, good Canterbury;
  Thy truth and thy integrity is rooted
  In us, thy friend. Give me thy hand; stand up.   115
  Prithee, let's walk. Now, by my holidame,°
  What manner of man are you? My lord, I looked
  You would have given me your petition, that
  I should have ta'en some pains to bring together
  Yourself and your accusers, and to have heard you, 120
  Without indurance further.°

Cranmer.   Most dread liege,
  The good I stand on is my truth and honesty.
  If they shall fail, I with mine enemies
  Will triumph o'er my person; which I weigh not,
  Being of those virtues vacant.° I fear nothing°   125
  What can be said against me.

King.   Know you not
  How your state stands i' th' world, with the whole
    world?
  Your enemies are many, and not small. Their prac-
    tices

---

106 make your house our Tow'r be housed in the Tower (cf.I.i.207)
106 You a brother of us i.e., you being a member of the council
110 throughly thoroughly   **111 corn** wheat   **112 stands under** subject to   **116 by my holidame** by my holiness (a formula of protesta-
tion)   **121 indurance further** (1) imprisonment in addition (2)
further hardship   **124–25 I weigh . . . vacant** I do not value if
it is devoid of those virtues (i.e., truth and honesty)   **125 nothing**
not at all

Must bear the same proportion,° and not ever°
130 The justice and the truth o' th' question carries
The due° o' th' verdict with it. At what ease°
Might corrupt minds procure knaves as corrupt
To swear against you? Such things have been done.
You are potently opposed, and with a malice
135 Of as great size. Ween you of° better luck—
I mean, in perjured witness°—than your master,°
Whose minister you are, whiles here he lived
Upon this naughty° earth? Go to, go to;
You take a precipice for no leap of danger,
And woo your own destruction.

140 *Cranmer*.   God and your Majesty
Protect mine innocence, or I fall into
The trap is° laid for me!

King.   Be of good cheer;
They shall no more prevail than we give way° to.
Keep comfort to you, and this morning see
145 You do appear before them. If they shall chance,
In charging you with matters, to commit you,°
The best persuasions to the contrary
Fail not to use, and with what vehemency
Th' occasion shall instruct you. If entreaties
150 Will render you no remedy, this ring
Deliver them, and your appeal to us
There make before them. Look, the good man
        weeps!
He's honest, on mine honor. God's blest mother,
I swear he is true-hearted, and a soul
155 None better in my kingdom. Get you gone,
And do as I have bid you. (*Exit Cranmer.*) He has
        strangled
His language in his tears.

128–29 **Their practices . . . proportion** their plots must correspond
in number and scope   129 **ever** always   131 **due** fit reward   131
At what ease how easily   135 **Ween you of** do you reckon on   136
witness evidence   136 **master** i.e., Christ   138 **naughty** wicked
142 **is** that is   143 **way** scope   146 **commit you** i.e., to imprisonment in the Tower

Enter Old Lady; [Lovell following].

Gentleman. (*Within.*) Come back: what mean you?

Old Lady. I'll not come back; the tidings that I bring
    Will make my boldness manners. Now, good angels
    Fly o'er thy royal head, and shade thy person   160
    Under their blessed wings!

King.   Now by thy looks
    I guess thy message. Is the Queen delivered?
    Say "aye," and of a boy.

Old Lady.   Aye, aye, my liege,
    And of a lovely boy. The God of heaven
    Both now and ever bless her! 'Tis a girl   165
    Promises boys hereafter. Sir, your Queen
    Desires your visitation, and to be
    Acquainted with this stranger. 'Tis as like you
    As cherry is to cherry.

King.   Lovell!

Lovell.   Sir?

King. Give her an hundred marks.° I'll to the Queen.   170
                                Exit King.

Old Lady. An hundred marks? By this light, I'll ha'
    more.
    An ordinary groom is for° such payment.
    I will have more, or scold it out of him.
    Said I for this, the girl was like to him? I'll
    Have more, or else unsay't; and now, while 'tis hot,   175
    I'll put it to the issue.   *[Exeunt.]*

---

170 **an hundred marks** (one mark = 13s.4d. [two-thirds of a pound];
a hundred marks = £66.13s.4d. a substantial sum) 172 **for** entitled to

Scene II. [*Before the entrance to the
council-chamber.*]

*Enter Cranmer, Archbishop of Canterbury; [pursui-
vants,° pages, etc., attending at the door].*

Cranmer. I hope I am not too late; and yet the gentle-
man
  That was sent to me from the council prayed me
  To make great haste. All fast?° What means this?
  Ho!
  Who waits there? Sure, you know me?

Enter Keeper.

Keeper.   Yes, my lord,
5   But yet I cannot help you.

Cranmer. Why?

Keeper. Your Grace must wait till you be called for.

Enter Doctor Butts.

Cranmer.   So.

Butts. [*Aside*] This is a piece of malice. I am glad
  I came this way so happily. The King
  Shall understand it presently.°   *Exit Butts.*

10 *Cranmer.* [*Aside*]   'Tis Butts,
  The King's physician. As he passed along,
  How earnestly he cast his eyes upon me.
  Pray heaven he sound° not my disgrace! For cer-
  tain,
  This is of purpose laid by some that hate me

V.ii.s.d. **pursuivants** junior officers attendant upon the heralds 3
fast shut 10 **understand it presently** know about it at once 13
sound (1) fathom (2) make known

(God turn° their hearts! I never sought their
   malice)   *15*
To quench mine honor. They would shame to make
   me
Wait else at door, a fellow-councillor,
'Mong boys, grooms, and lackeys. But their plea-
   sures
Must be fulfilled, and I attend with patience.

Enter the King and Butts at a window above.°

Butts. I'll show your Grace the strangest sight—   *20*

King.   What's that, Butts?

Butts. I think your Highness saw this many a day.

King. Body o' me, where is it?

Butts.   There, my lord:
The high promotion of his Grace of Canterbury,
Who holds his state° at door 'mongst pursuivants,
Pages, and footboys.

King.   Ha? 'Tis he, indeed.   *25*
Is this the honor they do one another?
'Tis well there's one above 'em yet. I had thought
They had parted so much honesty° among 'em,
At least good manners, as not thus to suffer
A man of his place and so near our favor   *30*
To dance attendance on their lordships' pleasures,
And at the door too, like a post with packets.°
By holy Mary, Butts, there's knavery.
Let 'em alone, and draw the curtain close;
We shall hear more anon.   *35*

[*They retire behind the curtain; Cranmer remains
waiting outside.*]

---

15 turn convert   **19 s.d. above** (i.e., on the upper stage; note the
reference to a curtain, line 34)   **24 holds his state** maintains the
dignity of his position   **28 parted so much honesty** shared enough
decency   **32 post with packets** courier with letters

[*Scene* III. *The council-chamber.*]

*A council-table brought in with chairs and stools, and
placed under the state.° Enter Lord Chancellor, places
himself at the upper end of the table on the left hand;
a seat being left void° above him, as for Canterbury's
seat. Duke of Suffolk, Duke of Norfolk, Surrey, Lord
Chamberlain, Gardiner, seat themselves in order on
each side. Cromwell at lower end, as secretary.*
[*Keeper at the door.*]

Chancellor. Speak to the business, master secretary.
   Why are we met in council?

Cromwell.   Please your honors,
   The chief cause concerns his Grace of Canterbury.

Gardiner. Has he had knowledge° of it?

Cromwell.   Yes.

Norfolk.   Who waits there?

Keeper. Without,° my noble lords?

Gardiner.   Yes.

5 *Keeper.*   My Lord Archbishop;
   And has done half an hour, to know your pleasures.

Chancellor. Let him come in.

Keeper.   Your Grace may enter now.

Cranmer [*enters and*] *approaches the council-table.*

Chancellor. My good Lord Archbishop, I'm very sorry
   To sit here at this present° and behold
10 That chair stand empty. But we all are men,

V.iii.s.d. **state** canopy **void** empty 4 **had knowledge** been informed 5 **Without** outside the door 9 **at this present** now

In our own natures frail and capable
Of° our flesh; few are angels: out of which frailty
And want of wisdom, you, that best should teach
     us,
Have misdemeaned yourself, and not a little,
Toward the King first, then his laws, in filling   15
The whole realm, by your teaching and your chap-
     lains'—
For so we are informed—with new opinions,
Divers and dangerous; which are heresies,
And, not reformed, may prove pernicious.°

Gardiner. Which reformation must be sudden too,   20
    My noble lords; for those that tame wild horses
    Pace 'em not in their hands° to make 'em gentle,
    But stop their mouths with stubborn° bits and spur
         'em
    Till they obey the manage.° If we suffer,
    Out of our easiness and childish pity   25
    To one man's honor, this contagious sickness,
    Farewell all physic. And what follows then?
    Commotions, uproars, with a general taint°
    Of the whole state; as of late days our neighbors,
    The upper Germany,° can dearly witness,   30
    Yet freshly pitied in our memories.

Cranmer. My good lords, hitherto, in all the progress
    Both of my life and office, I have labored,
    And with no little study, that my teaching
    And the strong course of my authority
    Might go one way, and safely; and the end   35
    Was ever to do well. Nor is there living
    (I speak it with a single heart,° my lords)
    A man that more detests, more stirs° against,
    Both in his private conscience and his place,   40

11–12 **capable/Of** i.e., susceptible to the weaknesses of   19 **pernicious** ruinous   22 **Pace 'em not in their hands** do not lead them
by hand through their paces   23 **stubborn** stiff, inflexible   24
manage training   28 **taint** corruption   30 **upper Germany** (possibly
referring to the peasants' uprising in Saxony in 1521–22 or to other
insurrections in 1524 and 1535)   38 **with a single heart** i.e., without
duplicity   39 **stirs** bestirs himself

Defacers of a public peace, than I do.
Pray heaven, the King may never find a heart
With less allegiance in it! Men that make
Envy and crookèd malice nourishment°
45   Dare bite the best. I do beseech your lordships
That, in this case of° justice, my accusers,
Be what they will, may stand forth face to face,
And freely urge° against me.

Suffolk.   Nay, my lord,
That cannot be. You are a councillor,
50   And, by that virtue,° no man dare accuse you.

Gardiner. My lord, because we have business of more
      moment,
We will be short with you. 'Tis his Highness' plea-
      sure,
And our consent,° for better trial of you,
From hence you be committed to the Tower;
55   Where, being but a private man° again,
You shall know many dare accuse you boldly,
More than, I fear, you are provided for.

Cranmer. Ah, my good Lord of Winchester, I thank
      you;
You are always my good friend. If your will pass,°
60   I shall both find your lordship° judge and juror,
You are so merciful. I see your end:
'Tis my undoing. Love and meekness, lord,
Become a churchman better than ambition.
Win straying souls with modesty° again;
65   Cast none away. That I shall clear myself,
Lay all the weight ye can upon my patience,
I make as little doubt as you do conscience°
In doing daily wrongs. I could say more,
But reverence to your calling makes me modest.

43–44 **make . . . nourishment** ("make nourishment" = feed on)   46
of involving   48 **urge** press their charges   50 **that virtue** virtue of
that   53 **our consent** what we have consented to   55 **private man**
i.e., without public office   59 **pass** prevail   60 **both find your lordship** find your lordship both   64 **modesty** moderation   67 **I make
. . . conscience** I have as little doubt as you have scruples

Gardiner. My lord, my lord, you are a sectary;°   *70*
   That's the plain truth. Your painted gloss dis-
     covers,°
   To men that understand you, words° and weakness.

Cromwell. My Lord of Winchester, y'are a little,
   By your good favor, too sharp. Men so noble,
   However faulty, yet should find respect   *75*
   For what they have been; 'tis a cruelty
   To load° a falling man.

Gardiner.   Good master secretary,
   I cry your honor mercy;° you may, worst°
   Of all this table, say so.

Cromwell.   Why, my lord?

Gardiner. Do not I know you for a favorer   *80*
   Of this new sect? Ye are not sound.°

Cromwell.   Not sound?

Gardiner. Not sound, I say.

Cromwell.   Would you were half so honest!
   Men's prayers then would seek you, not their fears.

Gardiner. I shall remember this bold language.

Cromwell.   Do.
   Remember your bold life too.

Chancellor.   This is too much;   *85*
   Forbear, for shame, my lords.

Gardiner.   I have done.

Cromwell.   And I.

Chancellor. Then thus for you, my lord: it stands
   agreed,
   I take it, by all voices, that forthwith

70 sectary follower of a (heretical) sect **71 painted gloss discovers**
deceitful appearance (or speech) reveals **72 words** i.e., rather than
content **77 load** oppress **78 cry your honor mercy** beg your
honor's pardon **78 worst** with least justification **81 sound** loyal

You be conveyed to th' Tower a prisoner,
90   There to remain till the King's further pleasure
Be known unto us. Are you all agreed, lords?

All. We are.

Cranmer.   Is there no other way of mercy,
But I must needs to th' Tower, my lords?

Gardiner.   What other
Would you expect? You are strangely° trouble-
    some.
Let some o' th' guard be ready there.

Enter the Guard.

95 *Cranmer.*   For me?
Must I go like a traitor thither?

Gardiner.   Receive him,
And see him safe i' th' Tower.

Cranmer.   Stay, good my lords,
I have a little yet to say. Look there, my lords.
By virtue of that ring, I take my cause
100   Out of the gripes° of cruel men, and give it
To a most noble judge, the King my master.

Chamberlain. This is the King's ring.

Surrey.   'Tis no counterfeit.

Suffolk. 'Tis the right ring, by heaven. I told ye all,
When we first put this dangerous stone arolling,
'Twould fall upon ourselves.

105 *Norfolk.*   Do you think, my lords,
The King will suffer but° the little finger
Of this man to be vexed?

Chamberlain.   'Tis now too certain.
How much more is his life in value with° him?
Would I were fairly out on't!

94 **strangely** uncommonly   100 **gripes** clutches   106 **suffer but** allow even   108 **in value with** esteemed by

Cromwell.   My mind gave° me,
  In seeking tales and informations   *110*
  Against this man, whose honesty the devil
  And his disciples only envy at,°
  Ye blew the fire that burns ye. Now have at ye!

Enter King, frowning on them; takes his seat.

Gardiner. Dread sovereign, how much are we bound
    to heaven
  In daily thanks, that gave us such a prince,   *115*
  Not only good and wise, but most religious;
  One that in all obedience makes the church
  The chief aim of his honor, and, to strengthen
  That holy duty, out of dear respect,°
  His royal self in judgment comes to hear   *120*
  The cause betwixt her and this great offender.

King. You were ever good at sudden commenda-
    tions,°
  Bishop of Winchester. But know, I come not
  To hear such flattery now, and in my presence
  They are too thin and bare to hide offenses.   *125*
  To me you cannot reach. You play the spaniel,
  And think with wagging of your tongue to win me;
  But, whatsoe'er thou tak'st me for, I'm sure
  Thou hast a cruel nature and a bloody.
  [*To Cranmer*] Good man, sit down. Now let me see
    the proudest,   *130*
  He that dares most, but wag his finger at thee.
  By all that's holy, he had better starve°
  Than but once think this place becomes thee not.

Surrey. May it please your Grace—

King.   No, sir, it does not please me.
  I had thought I had had men of some understand-
    ing   *135*
  And wisdom of my council, but I find none.

---

109 **gave** told   112 **envy at** hate   119 **dear respect** heartfelt care
(for the church)   122 **sudden commendations** extemporaneous compliments   132 **starve** die

Was it discretion, lords, to let this man,
This good man—few of you deserve that title—
This honest man, wait like a lousy° footboy
140 At chamber door? And one as great as you are?
Why, what a shame was this! Did my commission
Bid ye so far forget yourselves? I gave ye
Power as he was a councillor to try him,
Not as a groom. There's some of ye, I see,
145 More out of malice than integrity,
Would try him to the utmost, had ye mean;°
Which ye shall never have while I live.

Chancellor.   Thus far,
My most dread sovereign, may it like° your Grace
To let my tongue excuse all. What was purposed
150 Concerning his imprisonment was rather,
If there be faith in men, meant for his trial
And fair purgation° to the world, than malice,
I'm sure, in me.

King.   Well, well, my lords, respect him.
Take him and use him well; he's worthy of it.
155 I will say thus much for him, if a prince
May be beholding to a subject, I
Am, for his love and service, so to him.
Make me no more ado, but all embrace him.
Be friends, for shame, my lords! My Lord of Can-
    terbury,
160 I have a suit which you must not deny me:
That is, a fair young maid that yet wants° baptism;
You must be godfather, and answer for her.

Cranmer. The greatest monarch now alive may glory
In such an honor. How may I deserve it,
165 That am a poor and humble subject to you?

King. Come, come, my lord, you'd spare your
spoons.° You shall have two noble partners° with

139 **lousy** lice infested   146 **mean** means   148 **like** please   152
purgation vindication   161 **wants** lacks   166–67 **spare your spoons**
save the expense of giving spoons (traditional christening gifts)
167 **partners** co-sponsors

you: the old Duchess of Norfolk, and Lady
Marquess Dorset. Will these please you?
Once more, my Lord of Winchester, I charge you,   170
Embrace and love this man.

Gardiner.   With a true heart
And brother-love I do it.

Cranmer.   And let heaven
Witness how dear I hold this confirmation.

King. Good man, those joyful tears show thy true
     heart.
The common voice,° I see, is verified   175
Of thee, which says thus: "Do my Lord of Can-
     terbury
A shrewd° turn, and he's your friend forever."
Come, lords, we trifle time away. I long
To have this young one made a Christian.
As I have made ye one, lords, one remain;   180
So I grow stronger, you more honor gain.   *Exeunt.*

Scene [IV. *The palace yard.*]

Noise and tumult within. Enter Porter and his Man.

Porter. You'll leave your noise anon, ye rascals. Do
     you take the court for Parish Garden?° Ye rude°
     slaves, leave your gaping.°

(*Within.*) Good master porter, I belong to th' larder.°

Porter. Belong to th' gallows, and be hanged, ye   5
     rogue! Is this a place to roar in? Fetch me a dozen
     crab-tree staves, and strong ones: these are but

---

175 **common voice** popular report   177 **shrewd** nasty   V.iv.2 **Parish
Garden** Paris Garden, a boisterous bear-baiting arena on the Bank-
side   2 **rude** uncivilized   3 **leave your gaping** stop your bawling
4 **belong to th' larder** am employed in the (palace) pantry

switches to 'em.° I'll scratch your heads. You must
be seeing christenings? Do you look for ale and
10   cakes° here, you rude rascals?

Man. Pray, sir, be patient. 'Tis as much impossible,
Unless we sweep 'em from the door with cannons,
To scatter 'em, as 'tis to make 'em sleep
On May-Day° morning, which will never be.
15   We may as well push against Paul's° as stir 'em.

Porter. How got they in, and be hanged?

Man. Alas, I know not. How gets the tide in?
As much as one sound cudgel of four foot
(You see the poor remainder) could distribute,
I made no° spare, sir.

20   *Porter.*   You did nothing, sir.

Man. I am not Samson, nor Sir Guy, nor Colbrand,°
To mow 'em down before me; but if I spared any
That had a head to hit, either young or old,
He or she, cuckold or cuckold-maker,
25   Let me ne'er hope to see a chine° again;
And that I would not for a cow, God save her!°

(*Within.*) Do you hear, master porter?

Porter. I shall be with you° presently, good master
puppy. Keep the door close, sirrah.°

30   *Man.* What would you have me do?

Porter. What should you do, but knock 'em down by
th' dozens? Is this Moorfields° to muster in? Or

---

8 **switches to 'em** twigs in comparison   9–10 **ale and cakes** (traditional fare at christenings and other celebrations)   14 **May-Day**
(a holiday the celebration of which began before sunrise)   15
Paul's St. Paul's Cathedral   20 **made no** did not   21 **Samson, nor
Sir Guy, nor Colbrand** (all three possessed legendary strength;
Guy of Warwick was celebrated in romance for slaying the Danish
Giant Colbrand)   25 **see a chine** i.e., eat beef   26 **for a cow, God
save her** (a current expression of doubtful import; perhaps mean-
ingless)   28 **I shall be with you** I'll trounce you (Maxwell)   29
sirrah (term of address used to inferiors)   32 **Moorfields** a recreation field on the London outskirts

have we some strange Indian with the great tool°
come to court, the women so besiege us? Bless me,
what a fry of fornication° is at door! On my Chris-   *35*
tian conscience, this one christening will beget a
thousand; here will be father, godfather, and all together.

Man. The spoons° will be the bigger, sir. There is
a fellow somewhat near the door, he should be a   *40*
brazier by his face,° for, o' my conscience, twenty
of the dog days° now reign in's nose. All that stand
about him are under the line;° they need no other
penance. That firedrake° did I hit three times on
the head, and three times was his nose discharged   *45*
against me; he stands there, like a mortarpiece,° to
blow us.° There was a haberdasher's wife of small
wit near him, that railed upon me till her pinked
porringer° fell off her head, for kindling such a
combustion in the state. I missed the meteor once,   *50*
and hit that woman, who cried out "Clubs!"° when
I might see from far some forty truncheoners° draw
to her succor, which were the hope o' th' Strand,°
where she was quartered. They fell on; I made
good° my place. At length they came to th' broom-   *55*
staff° to me. I defied 'em still; when suddenly a
file° of boys behind 'em, loose shot,° delivered such
a show'r of pebbles, that I was fain° to draw mine

---

33 **some strange Indian with the great tool** (American Indians were
exhibited at court; "tool" = penis)   35 **fry of fornication** (1)
swarm of would-be fornicators (2) swarming offspring of fornication   39 **spoons** (cf. V.iii. 166–67)   41 **brazier by his face** brass-
worker by his (red) face   42 **dog days** (the period from about July
3 to August 15, when Sirius, the Dog Star, rises at almost the
same time as the sun; regarded as the hottest and most unwhole-
some season of the year)   43 **line** equator   44 **firedrake** (1) fiery
dragon (2) meteor   46 **mortarpiece** squat cannon with a large bore
47 **blow us** blow us up   48–49 **pinked porringer** round cap with scal-
loped edge or ornamental perforations   51 **Clubs** (the rallying cry
of the London apprentices)   52 **truncheoners** truncheon (or cudgel)
bearers   53 **were the hope o' th' Strand** i.e., belonged to the shops
in the Strand, in Jacobean times a fashionable street   54–55 **They
fell on; I made good** they attacked; I defended   55–56 **to th' broom-
staff** i.e., to close quarters   57 **file** small company   57 **loose shot**
unaffiliated marksmen   58 **fain** obliged

honor in and let 'em win the work.° The devil was
60 amongst 'em, I think, surely.

Porter. These are the youths that thunder at a playhouse and fight for bitten apples; that no audience
but the tribulation° of Tower Hill° or the limbs° of
Limehouse,° their dear brothers, are able to en-
65 dure. I have some of 'em in Limbo Patrum,° and
there they are like to dance these three days; besides the running banquet of two beadles° that is
to come.

Enter Lord Chamberlain.

Chamberlain. Mercy o' me, what a multitude are here!
70 They grow still too; from all parts they are coming,
As if we kept a fair here. Where are these porters,
These lazy knaves? Y'have made a fine hand, fel-
lows;
There's a trim° rabble let in. Are all these
Your faithful friends o' th' suburbs?° We shall have
75 Great store of room, no doubt, left for the ladies,
When they pass back from the christening.

Porter.   And't please your honor,
We are but men; and what so many may do,
Not being torn apieces, we have done.
An army cannot rule 'em.

Chamberlain.   As I live,
80 If the King blame me for't, I'll lay ye all
By th' heels, and suddenly;° and on your heads
Clap round° fines for neglect. Y'are lazy knaves,
And here ye lie baiting of bombards° when
Ye should do service. Hark! The trumpets sound;

59 **work** fort   63 **tribulation** troublemakers   63 **Tower Hill** an un-
ruly district   63 **limbs** inhabitants, with a possible reference to
the limbs of the devil   64 **Limehouse** the rough dockyard area   65
Limbo Patrum i.e., prison (literally the underworld abode of the
souls of the just who died before Christ's coming)   67 **running
banquet of two beadles** i.e., a public whipping, as a dessert to the
"feast" of their confinement   73 **trim** fine   74 **suburbs** disreputable
districts outside City jurisdiction   80–81 **I'll lay . . . suddenly** I'll
have you all put straightaway into fetters   82 **round** stiff   83 **baiting of bombards** drinking from leather jugs

Th'are come already from the christening.   85
Go, break among the press,° and find a way out
To let the troop pass fairly, or I'll find
A Marshalsea° shall hold ye play these two months.

Porter. Make way there for the Princess.

Man.   You great fellow,
Stand close up, or I'll make your head ache.   90

Porter. You i' th' camlet,° get up o' th' rail;
I'll peck you o'er the pales° else.   *Exeunt.*

Scene [V. *The palace.*]

*Enter trumpets, sounding; then two Aldermen, Lord
Mayor, Garter,° Cranmer, Duke of Norfolk with his
marshal's staff, Duke of Suffolk, two Noblemen bearing great standing-bowls° for the christening gifts;
then four Noblemen bearing a canopy, under which
the Duchess of Norfolk, godmother, bearing the child
richly habited in a mantle, etc., train borne by a
Lady. Then follows the Marchioness Dorset, the other
godmother, and Ladies. The troop pass once about
the stage, and Garter speaks.*

Garter. Heaven, from thy endless goodness, send
    prosperous life, long, and ever happy, to the high
    and mighty Princess of England, Elizabeth!

Flourish. Enter King and Guard.

Cranmer. [*Kneeling*] And to your royal Grace and the
    good Queen.

86 **press** throng   88 **Marshalsea** prison in Southwark   91 **camlet**
a rich fabric made of Angora wool and other materials   92 **peck
you o'er the pales** pitch you over the palings   V.v.s.d. **Garter** (see
IV.i.36s.d., and note)   **standing-bowls** i.e., bowls with supporting
legs or base

5   My noble partners° and myself thus pray:
       All comfort, joy, in this most gracious lady
       Heaven ever laid up to make parents happy
       May hourly fall upon ye!

King.   Thank you, good Lord Archbishop.
       What is her name?

Cranmer.   Elizabeth.

King.   Stand up, lord.
                    [*The King kisses the child.*]
10   With this kiss take my blessing: God protect thee!
       Into whose hand I give thy life.

Cranmer.   Amen.

King. My noble gossips,° y'have been too prodigal.°
       I thank ye heartily; so shall this lady,
       When she has so much English.

Cranmer.   Let me speak, sir,
15   For heaven now bids me; and the words I utter
       Let none think flattery, for they'll find 'em truth.
       This royal infant—heaven still° move about her!—
       Though in her cradle, yet now promises
       Upon this land a thousand thousand blessings,
20   Which time shall bring to ripeness. She shall be
       (But few now living can behold that goodness)
       A pattern to all princes living with her
       And all that shall succeed. Saba° was never
       More covetous of wisdom and fair virtue
25   Than this pure soul shall be. All princely graces
       That mold up such a mighty piece° as this is,
       With all the virtues that attend the good,
       Shall still be doubled on her. Truth shall nurse her,
       Holy and heavenly thoughts still counsel her.
       She shall be loved and feared. Her own° shall bless
30   her;

5 **partners** co-sponsors   12 **gossips** godparents   12 **prodigal** generous with gifts   17 **still** always   23 **Saba** the Queen of Sheba   26
mold up such a mighty piece go to form so great a personage
30 **own** i.e., own people

Her foes shake like a field of beaten corn,°
And hang their heads with sorrow. Good grows
  with her;
In her days every man shall eat in safety
Under his own vine what he plants, and sing
The merry songs of peace to all his neighbors.   35
God shall be truly known, and those about her
From her shall read° the perfect ways of honor,
And by those claim their greatness, not by blood.
Nor shall this peace sleep with her; but as when
The bird of wonder dies, the maiden phoenix,°   40
Her ashes new create another heir
As great in admiration° as herself,
So shall she leave her blessedness to one°
(When heaven shall call her from this cloud of
  darkness)
Who from the sacred ashes of her honor   45
Shall star-like rise, as great in fame as she was,
And so stand fixed.° Peace, plenty, love, truth,
  terror,
That were the servants to this chosen infant,
Shall then be his, and like a vine grow to him.
Wherever the bright sun of heaven shall shine,   50
His honor and the greatness of his name
Shall be, and make new nations. He shall flourish,
And like a mountain cedar reach his branches
To all the plains about him.° Our children's chil-
  dren
Shall see this, and bless heaven.

King.   Thou speakest wonders.   55

Cranmer. She shall be, to the happiness of England,
  An agèd princess; many days shall see her,
  And yet no day without a deed to crown it.

31 **corn** wheat   37 **read** learn   40 **phoenix** the fabled Arabian bird
—unique in all the world—that after a life of 660 years rises anew
from the ashes in which it has consumed itself   42 **admiration**
"ability to excite wonder" (Foakes)   43 **one** i.e., James I   47 **fixed**
i.e., as a fixed star   50–54 **Wherever . . . about him** (inspired by
a prophecy in Genesis 17:4–6 which was often cited in connection
with Princess Elizabeth's marriage in 1613 [Foakes]; the "new
nations" may allude to the colonization of Virginia)

Would I had known no more! But she must die:
60 She must, the saints must have her. Yet a virgin,
A most unspotted lily, shall she pass
To th' ground, and all the world shall mourn her.

King. O Lord Archbishop,
Thou hast made me now a man; never before
65 This happy child did I get° anything.
This oracle of comfort has so pleased me
That when I am in heaven I shall desire
To see what this child does, and praise my Maker.
I thank ye all. To you, my good Lord Mayor,
70 And your good brethren, I am much beholding;
I have received much honor by your presence,
And ye shall find me thankful. Lead the way, lords.
Ye must all see the Queen, and she must thank ye;
She will be sick else. This day, no man think°
75 Has° business at his house; for all shall stay:°
This little one shall make it holiday.   *Exeunt.*

THE EPILOGUE

'Tis ten to one this play can never please
All that are here. Some come to take their ease,
And sleep an act or two; but those, we fear,
W'have frighted with our trumpets; so, 'tis clear,
5 They'll say 'tis naught;° others, to hear the city
Abused extremely, and to cry "That's witty!"°
Which we have not done neither; that,° I fear,
All the expected good w'are like to hear
For this play at this time, is only in
10 The merciful construction° of good women,
For such a one we showed 'em. If they smile
And say 'twill do, I know, within a while
All the best men are ours; for 'tis ill hap°
If they hold when their ladies bid 'em clap.

FINIS

65 **get** beget   74 **no man think** let no man think   75 **Has** he has   75
stay stop   Epilogue   5 **naught** worthless   5–6 **others . . . witty** (a
glance at the vogue for satirical comedies of London life)   7 **that**
so that   10 **construction** interpretation   13 **hap** luck

Textual Note

The Famous History of the Life of King Henry the Eighth did not achieve publication until seven years after Shakespeare's death, when it appeared in the collected First Folio of his works as the last of the history plays. The 1623 Folio furnishes the only authoritative early edition of *Henry VIII*. Fortunately it is a very good one: behind the Folio text apparently lies a careful scribal transcription of the authors'—or author's—own manuscript. To the playwright(s), rather than the prompter, we presumably owe the very full stage directions called for by a spectacular historical drama. With few exceptions, entrances and exits are fully indicated. Speech prefixes are throughout correct and unambiguous, except for confusion of the First and Second Gentleman at IV.i.20–23 and 55, and of the Lord Chamberlain with the Lord Chancellor at V.iii.85 and 87. Indeed the text as a whole is very clean and straightforward, with relatively little corruption or error of any kind, although the language—often complex in Shakespeare's mature manner—not surprisingly presents a number of interpretative problems.

The Folio text directly or indirectly provides the basis for all subsequent editions of *Henry VIII*. Wherever possible the present edition reproduces it, modernizing spelling, and altering punctuation and verse lineations where the editor's sense of literary and dramatic fitness dictated. The Latin act and scene divisions of the Folio have been translated, and a new division (as in the Globe text) is introduced after V.ii.35. Consequently, in the fifth act the Folio's *Scena Tertia* and *Scena Quarta* are rendered as

V.iv and V.v respectively. Abbreviations have been expanded and speech prefixes regularized. Stage directions have been amplified where necessary, such additions being printed within square brackets. Obvious typographical errors have been corrected and eccentric spellings regularized where appropriate without notice, but all significant emendations are noted below. In this list the adopted reading is given in italics and is followed by the rejected Folio reading in roman type or a note of the Folio's omission within square brackets.

I.i.42–45 *All . . . function* [F assigns to Buckingham]   47 *as you guess* [F assigns to Norfolk]   63 *web, 'a* Web. O   69–70 *that? . . . hell, that, . . .* Hell?   183 *He* [F omits]   200 *Hereford* Hertford   219 *Parke* Pecke   221 *Nicholas* Michaell   227 *lord* Lords
I.ii.156 *feared* feare   164 *confession's* Commissions   170 *win* [F omits]   180 *To* For this to   190 *Bulmer* Blumer
I.iii.12 *saw* see   13 *Or* A   59 *wherewithal. In him* wherewithall in him;

II.i.20 *Parke* Pecke   86 *mark* make
II.iii.14 *quarrel,* quarrell.   61 *you* you, to you
II.iv.174 *A* And   319 *summons. Unsolicited* Summons vnsolicited.

III.i.21 *coming, now I think on't.* comming; now I thinke on't,   23s.d. *Campeius* Campian   61 *your* our
III.ii.142 *glad* gald   171 *filed* fill'd   292 *Who* Whom   343 *Chattels* Castles

IV.i.20–23 *I thank . . . business?* [F assigns to First Gentleman]   34 *Kimbolton* Kymmalton   55 *And sometimes falling ones.* [F assigns to Second Gentleman]   101 *Stokesly* Stokeley
IV.ii.7 *think* thanke   50 *honor from* Honor. From

V.i.24 *thee* the   37 *time* Lime   139 *precipice* Precepit   176s.d. *[Exeunt.]* Exit Ladie.
V.ii.8 *piece* Peere
V.iii.85–86 *This . . . lords.* [F assigns to Lord Chamberlain]   87–91 *Then . . . agreed, lords?* [F assigns to Lord Chamberlain]   125 *bare* base   133 *this* his   174 *heart* hearts
V.v.37 *ways* way   70 *your* you

The Sources of *Henry VIII*

The chief sources for the play, as for Shakespeare's great earlier cycle of historical dramas on the reigns of the English monarchs from Richard II through Richard III, is Raphael Holinshed's *Chronicles of England, Scotland, and Ireland* (2nd ed., 1587). It is depended upon throughout, except for the story of the plot against Cranmer, and his vindication, in Act V; here the authority, closely followed, is John Foxe's *Acts and Monuments,* the enlarged 1570 version of which went through a number of editions before the close of the century. Whether the playwright(s) also profited from other narrative chronicles is matter for speculation: the phraseological parallels adduced by scholars are often less than striking, and it is well known that the chroniclers themselves borrowed from one another freely. But Edward Hall's *Union of the Two Noble and Illustre Families of Lancaster and York* (1542) may have been consulted, and it is possible—although not demonstrable—that Wolsey's images of the star past its meridian and of the bladder of pride (III.ii.222–27, 359–62) derive from John Speed's *History of Great Britain* (1611). More persuasive is the evidence that the author(s) knew Samuel Rowley's boisterously farcical and blithely anachronistic drama on Henry's reign, *When You See Me You Know Me,* printed in 1605 and perhaps revived before being reprinted in 1613—the probable year of first performance for *Henry VIII.* The sneering references in the latter to "a merry bawdy play" consisting of "fool and fight" (Prologue 14–19) may allude to *When You See Me,* which nevertheless seems to have provided some minor inspiration, most notably in Henry's persistent ejaculation, "Ha!", used in both works. A significant indirect source is George Cavendish's *Life of Wolsey*, which, although not published until 1641, was utilized by the chroniclers from Stow (1565) onwards.

But of the direct and continuous dependence on Holinshed in *Henry VIII* there can be no question. The historical events of the play, from the Field of the Cloth of Gold in 1520 to the christening of Princess Elizabeth in 1533, cover roughly a third of Henry's long reign (1509–47). Four great episodes dominate this segment of Holinshed's narrative: Buckingham's fall, the divorce, Wolsey's disgrace, and the King's remarriage, culminating in the christening of the future queen. So too do they dominate the play. The source was evidently read with great care. At times, as in Katherine's long speech (II.iv.12–57), the dramatic blank verse is the prose of the *Chronicles* paraphrased (although even here there are significant additions). Holinshed is levied upon also for the elaborate stage directions for the ceremonial entries and processions in II.iv, IV.i, and V.v.

If adherence to the source was close, it was not, however, slavish. The abundant material of the *Chronicles* is winnowed, rearranged, and combined in accordance with the necessities of the dramatic design. Certain changes were dictated by limitations of stage personnel: the pageantry of the coronation, calling for a multitude of supernumeraries, had to be reduced. Other alterations are more substantive. Holinshed's account of the unfortunate Bishop of Durham who mistakenly sent the King a book documenting his private affairs, and thus enabled Wolsey to destroy him, is transferred to the Cardinal himself (III.ii. 120ff.). In the play the first hint of the King's attraction to Anne Bullen precedes Buckingham's execution, and is manifested at a feast which, with nice artistic economy, also illustrates the lavish scale on which Wolsey lives (I.iv). Historically, the King set his affections on Anne eight years after the execution, and she does not appear in Holinshed's description of the revel at York House that provides the basis for this scene.

Perhaps the most interesting transformations involve the portrayal of character. It is true that the King remains, in play as in chronicle, the exemplary monarch whose motives, unlike those of lesser mortals, are never critically examined. But on the stage his moments of anger or of withdrawal into pensiveness reveal facets of the smiling or stern public figure that Holinshed does not attempt to suggest. So, too, the Henry of the play gains in authority in the course of the action; hoodwinked by Wolsey in the earlier scenes, he is nobody's fool in Act V. Again the source offers no precedent. In the play the fallen Wolsey is invested with a pathos and dignity only barely hinted at in the chronicle. Katherine is endowed by the dramatist(s) with greater strength and regality than she displays in Holinshed, an effect in part achieved by such devices as her fearless—if unavailing—defense of Buckingham and accusations against the Cardinal in the King's presence (I.ii.9ff.).

These and other instances of the means by which prosaic historical narrative is transformed into complex poetic drama may be seen in the copious extracts from the relevant passages of Holinshed and Foxe which follow.

RAPHAEL HOLINSHED

from *Chronicles of England, Scotland, and Ireland* (1587 edition)

[III.ii.120–30] This year [1508] was Thomas Ruthall made Bishop of Durham. . . .

To whom . . . the King gave in charge to write a book of the whole estate of the kingdom. . . .

Afterwards the King commanded Cardinal Wolsey to go to this bishop, and to bring the book away with him to deliver to his Majesty. But see the mishap! That a man in all other things so provident should now be so negligent. . . . For this bishop, having written two books (the one to answer the King's command, and the other intreating of [i.e., dealing with] his own private affairs), did bind them both after one sort in vellum, . . . as the one could not by any especial note be discerned from the other. . . .

Now when the Cardinal came to demand the book due to the King, the Bishop unadvisedly commanded his servant to bring him the book bound in white vellum. . . . The servant . . . brought forth . . . the book intreating of the state of the Bishop, and delivered the same unto his master, who . . . gave it to the Cardinal to bear unto the King. The Cardinal . . . , understanding the contents thereof, he greatly rejoiced, having now occasion . . . to bring the Bishop into the King's disgrace.

Wherefore he went forthwith to the King, delivered the book into his hands, and briefly informed the King of the contents thereof; putting further into the King's head, that if at any time he were destitute of a mass of money, he should not need to seek further therefore than to the coffers of the Bishop, who by the tenor of his own book had accompted his proper riches and substance to the value of a hundred thousand pounds. Of all which when the Bishop had intelligence . . . he was stricken with such grief . . . that he shortly through extreme sorrow ended his life at London. . . .

[II.i.5–41] During this time [of the delivery of Tournai to the French king in 1520] remained in the French court divers young gentlemen of England, and they with the French king rode daily disguised through Paris, throwing eggs, stones, and other foolish trifles at the people; which light demeanor of a king was much discommended and jested at. And when these young gentlemen came again into England, they were all French in eating, drinking, and apparel, yea, and in French vices and brags, so that all the estates of England were by them laughed at. The ladies and gentlewomen were dispraised, so that nothing by them was praised, but if it were after the French turn, which after turned them to displeasure, as you shall hear. . . .

Then the King's council caused the Lord Chamberlain to call before them divers of the privy chamber, which had been in the French court, and banished them the court for divers considerations, laying nothing particularly to their charges . . . which discharge out of court grieved sore the hearts of these young men, which were called the King's minions. . . .

[I.ii.189–92] . . . the King specially rebuked Sir William Bulmer, Kt., because he, being his servant sworn, refused the King's service, and became servant to the Duke of Buckingham. . . .

[I.i.1ff.] The French king, desirous to continue the friendship lately begun betwixt him and the king of England, made means unto the Cardinal that they might in some convenient place come to an interview together. . . . But the fame went that the Cardinal desired greatly, of himself, that the two kings might meet, who, measuring by his will what was convenient, thought it should make much with his glory if in France also at some high assembly of noblemen he should be seen in his vain pomp and show of dignity ... and thus with his persuasions the King began to conceive an earnest desire to see the French king, and thereupon appointed to go over to Calais, and so in the marches of Guisnes to meet with him. . . .

Herewith were letters written to all such lords, ladies, gentlemen, and gentlewomen, which should give their attendance on the King and Queen, which incontinently put themselves in a readiness after the most sumptuous sort. Also it was appointed that the king of England and the French king, in a camp between Ard and Guisnes, with eighteen aides, should in June next ensuing abide all comers, being gentlemen, at the tilt, at tourney, and at barriers. . . .

... both the kings committed the order and manner of their meeting, and how many days the same should continue, and what preëminence each should give to other, unto the Cardinal of York, which, to set all things in a certainty, made an instrument containing an order and direction concerning the premises by him devised and appointed. . . .

The peers of the realm—receiving letters to prepare themselves to attend the King in this journey, and no apparent necessary cause expressed, why nor wherefore—seemed to grudge that such a costly journey should be taken in hand to their importunate charges and expenses, without consent of the whole board of the council. But namely the Duke of Buckingham, being a man of a lofty courage but not most liberal, sore repined that he should be at so great charges for his furniture forth at this time, saying that he knew not for what cause so much money should be spent about the sight of a vain talk to be had, and communication to be ministered of things of no importance; wherefore he sticked not to say that it was an intolerable matter to obey such a vile and importunate person. . . .

Now such grievous words as the Duke thus uttered against

him came to the Cardinal's ear, whereupon he cast before-
hand all ways possible to have him in a trip, that he might
cause him to leap headless. But because he doubted his
friends, kinsmen, and allies, and chiefly the Earl of Surrey,
Lord Admiral, which had married the Duke's daughter,
he thought good first to send him some whither out of
the way, lest he might cast a trump in his way. . . .

At length there was occasion offered him to compass
his purpose, by occasion of the Earl of Kildare his coming
out of Ireland. . . . Such accusations were framed against
him . . . that he was committed to prison, and then by the
Cardinal's good preferment the Earl of Surrey was sent
into Ireland as the King's deputy, in lieu of the said Earl
of Kildare, there to remain rather as an exile than as
lieutenant to the King, even at the Cardinal's pleasure, as
he himself well perceived. . . .

[I.ii.171–76] Now it chanced that the Duke . . . went . . .
into Kent unto a manor place which he had there. And
whilst he stayed in that country . . . , grievous complaints
were exhibited to him by his farmers and tenants against
Charles Knevet, his surveyor, for such bribing as he had
used there amongst them; whereupon the Duke took such
displeasure against him that he deprived him of his office,
not knowing how that in so doing he procured his own
destruction, as after appeared. . . .

[I.i.176–93] [The Emperor Charles V visited England
to see his aunt, the Queen, "of whom ye may be sure he
was most joyfully received and welcomed."] The chief
cause that moved the Emperor to come thus on land at
this time was to persuade that, by word of mouth, which
he had before done most earnestly by letters; which was,
that the King should not meet with the French king at any
interview: for he doubted lest if the king of England and
the French king should grow into some great friendship
and faithful bond of amity, it might turn him to displeasure.

But now that he perceived how the King was forward
on his journey, he did what he could to procure that no
trust should be committed to the fair words of the Frenchmen; and that, if it were possible, the great friendship

that was now in breeding betwixt the two kings might be dissolved. And forsomuch as he knew the Lord Cardinal to be won with rewards, as a fish with a bait, he bestowed on him great gifts, and promised him much more, so that he would be his friend, and help to bring his purpose to pass. The Cardinal ... promised to the Emperor that he would so use the matter as his purpose should be sped. ...

[I.i.6–45] The day of the meeting [of the Field of the Cloth of Gold] was appointed to be on the Thursday, the seventh of June, upon which day the two kings met in the vale of Andren, accompanied with such a number of the nobility of both realms, so richly appointed in apparel and costly jewels, as chains, collars of S's, and other the like ornaments to set forth their degrees and estates, that a wonder it was to behold and view them in their order and rooms, which every man kept according to his appointment.

The two kings meeting in the field, either saluted other in most loving wise, first on horseback, and after alighting on foot eftsoons embraced with courteous words, to the great rejoicing of the beholders; and after they had thus saluted each other, they went both together into a rich tent of cloth of gold, ... till it drew toward the evening, and then departed for that night, the one to Guisnes, the other to Ard. ... [A description of the tilting follows.]

Thus, course after course each with other, his counter party, did right valiantly, but the two kings surmounted all the rest in prowess and valiantness. ...

[I.i.89–94] On Monday, the eighteenth of June, was such an hideous storm of wind and weather, that many conjectured it did prognosticate trouble and hatred shortly after to follow between princes.

[I.i.212–26, I.ii.129–214] [In 1521] the Cardinal, boiling in hatred against the Duke of Buckingham and thirsting for his blood, devised to make Charles Knevet, that had been the Duke's surveyor, ... an instrument to bring the Duke to destruction. This Knevet, being had in examination before the Cardinal, disclosed all the Duke's life. And first he uttered, that the Duke was accustomed, by way of talk, to say how he meant so to use the matter, that he would attain to the crown if King Henry chanced to die without issue; and that he had talk and conference of that matter on a time with George Nevill, Lord of Abergavenny, unto whom he had given his daughter in marriage; and also that he threatened to punish the Cardinal for his manifold misdoings, being without cause his mortal enemy.

The Cardinal, having gotten that which he sought for, ... procured Knevet, with many comfortable words and great promises, that he should with a bold spirit and countenance object and lay these things to the Duke's charge, with more if he knew it when time required. Then Knevet, partly provoked with desire to be revenged and partly moved with hope of reward, openly confessed that the Duke had once fully determined to devise means how to make the King away, being brought into a full hope that he should be king by a vain prophecy which one Nicholas Hopkins, a monk of an house of the Chartreux order beside Bristow, called Henton, sometime his confessor, had opened unto him.

The Cardinal, having thus taken the examination of Knevet, went unto the King and declared unto him that his person was in danger by such traitorous purpose as the Duke of Buckingham had conceived in his heart, ... wherefore he exhorted the King to provide for his own surety with speed. The King ... enforced to the uttermost by the Cardinal, made this answer: "If the Duke have deserved to be punished, let him have according to his deserts." The Duke ... was straightways attached, and brought to the Tower by Sir Henry Marney, Captain of the Guard. . . . There was also attached the foresaid Chartreux monk, Master John de la Car *alias* de la Court, the Duke's confessor, and Sir Gilbert Perke, priest, the Duke's chancellor.

... inquisitions were taken in divers shires of England of him, so that by the knights and gentlemen he was indicted of high treason, for certain words spoken ... by the same Duke ... to the Lord of Abergavenny; and therewith was the same lord attached for concealment, and so likewise was the Lord Montacute, and both led to the Tower.... [There follows a listing of the "divers points of high treason" in the indictment against Buckingham.]

... the same Duke ... said unto one Charles Knevet, Esq., after that the King had reproved the Duke for retaining William Bulmer, Kt., into his service, that if he had perceived that he should have been committed to the Tower ... he would have played the part which his father intended to have put in practice against King Richard the Third at Salisbury, who made earnest suit to have come unto the presence of the same King Richard; which suit if he might have obtained, he having a knife secretly about him, would have thrust it into the body of King Richard, as he had made semblance to kneel down before him. And, in speaking these words, he maliciously laid his hand upon his dagger, and said that, if he were so evil used, he would do his best to accomplish his pretensed purpose, swearing to confirm his word by the blood of our Lord.

Beside all this, the same Duke ... at London in a place called the Rose, within the parish of St. Lawrence Poultney ... demanded of the said Charles Knevet, Esq., what was the talk amongst the Londoners concerning the King's journey beyond the seas? And the said Charles told him that many stood in doubt of that journey, lest the Frenchmen meant some deceit towards the King. Whereto the Duke answered, that it was to be feared, lest it would come to pass, according to the words of a certain holy monk: "For there is" (saith he), "a Chartreux monk that divers times hath sent to me, willing me to send unto him my chancellor; and I did send unto him John de la Court, my chaplain, unto whom he would not declare anything till de la Court had sworn unto him to keep all things secret, and to tell no creature living what he should hear of him, except it were to me.

"And then the said monk told de la Court that neither the King nor his heirs should prosper, and that I should endeavor myself to purchase the good wills of the commonalty of England, for I, the same Duke, and my blood should prosper, and have the rule of the realm of England." Then said Charles Knevet, "The monk may be deceived through the devil's illusion," and that it was evil to meddle with such matters. "Well," said the Duke, "it cannot hurt me," and so (saith the indictment) the Duke seemed to rejoice in the monk's words. And further, at the same time, the Duke told the said Charles that, if the King had miscarried now in his last sickness, he would have chopped off the heads of the Cardinal, of Sir Thomas Lovell, Kt., and of others; and also said that he had rather die for it than to be used as he had been. . . .

[II.i.1–140] . . . the Cardinal chiefly procured the death of this nobleman, no less favored and beloved of the people of this realm in that season than the Cardinal himself was hated and envied; which thing caused the Duke's fall the more to be pitied and lamented, sith he was the man of all other that chiefly went about to cross the Cardinal in his lordly demeanor and heady proceedings. . . . Shortly after that the Duke had been indicted . . . he was arraigned in Westminster Hall. . . .

When the lords had taken their place, the Duke was brought to the bar, and upon his arraignment pleaded not guilty, and put himself upon his peers. Then was his indictment read, which the Duke denied to be true, and (as he was an eloquent man) alleged reasons to falsify the indictment; pleading the matter for his own justification very pithily and earnestly. The King's attorney against the Duke's reasons alleged the examinations, confessions, and proofs of witnesses.

The Duke desired that the witnesses might be brought forth. And then came before him Charles Knevet, Perke, de la Court, and Hopkins the monk . . . which like a false hypocrite had induced the Duke to the treason with his false, forged prophecies. Divers presumptions and accusations were laid unto him by Charles Knevet, which he would fain have covered. The depositions were read, and the deponents delivered as prisoners to the officers of the Tower. . . .

[The peers conferred.] The Duke was brought to the bar sore chafing, and sweat marvellously; and after he had made his reverence, he paused a while. The Duke of

Norfolk, as judge, said: "Sir Edward, you have heard how you be indicted of high treason. You pleaded thereto not guilty, putting yourself to the peers of the realm, which have found you guilty." Then the Duke of Norfolk wept and said, "You shall be led to the King's prison and there laid on a hurdle, and so drawn to the place of execution, and there be hanged. . . ."

The Duke of Buckingham said: "My lord of Norfolk, you have said as a traitor should be said unto, but I was never any; but my lords I nothing malign for that you have done to me, but the eternal God forgive you my death, and I do. I shall never sue to the King for life, howbeit he is a gracious prince, and more grace may come from him than I desire. I desire you my lords, and all my fellows, to pray for me." Then was the edge of the ax turned towards him, and he led into a barge. Sir Thomas Lovell desired him to sit on the cushions and carpet ordained for him. He said, "Nay: for when I went to Westminster I was Duke of Buckingham; now I am but Edward Bohun, the most caitiff of the world." Thus they landed at the Temple, where received him Sir Nicholas Vaux and Sir William Sands, Bts., and led him through the city, who desired ever the people to pray for him, of whom some wept and lamented. . . .

[The Duke was led to the scaffold,] where he said he had offended the King's Grace through negligence and lack of grace, and desired all noblemen to beware by him, and all men to pray for him, and that he trusted to die the King's true man. Thus meekly with an ax he took his death. . . .

[There follows "A convenient collection concerning the High Constables of England," an office which Buckingham and his father were the last to hold.]

[I.i.200; II.i.53, 107–24] Henry Stafford . . . was High Constable of England, and Duke of Buckingham. This man, raising war against Richard the Third usurping the crown, was in the first year of the reign of the said Richard . . . betrayed by his man Humphrey Banister (to whom being in distress he fled for succor) and . . . was beheaded without arraignment or judgment. . . .

Edward Stafford, son to Henry . . . , being also Duke of Buckingham after the death of his father, was Constable of England, Earl of Hereford, Stafford, and North-ampton. . . . He is termed . . . the flower and mirror of all courtesy. This man . . . was by Henry the Seventh restored to his father's inheritance, in recompense of the loss of his father's life. . . .

[I.ii.20–108] The King [in 1525] being determined . . . to make wars in France, . . . by the Cardinal there was devised strange commissions, and sent . . . into every shire, . . . that the sixth part of every man's substance should be paid in money or plate to the King without delay, for the furniture of his war. Hereof followed such cursing, weeping, and exclamation against both King and Cardinal, that pity it was to hear. . . .

The Duke of Suffolk, sitting in commission about this subsidy in Suffolk, persuaded by courteous means the rich clothiers to assent thereto; but when they came home, and went about to discharge and put from them their spinners, carders, fullers, weavers, and other artificers, . . . the people began to assemble in companies. . . . The rage of the people increased. . . . And herewith there assembled together after the manner of rebels four thousand men. . . .

The King . . . assembled . . . a great council, in the which he openly protested that his mind was never to ask anything of his commons which might sound to the breach of his laws, wherefore he willed to know by whose means the commissions were so strictly given forth. . . .

The Cardinal excused himself, and said that . . . by the consent of the whole council it was done. . . . The King indeed was much offended. . . . Therefore he . . . caused letters to be sent into all shires, that the matter should no further be talked of; and he pardoned all them that had denied the demand openly or secretly. The Cardinal, to deliver himself of the evil will of the commons, . . . caused it to be bruited abroad that through his inter-cession the King had pardoned and released all things. . . .

[II.i.147–67; II.ii.89–106; III.ii.85–86; II.iv] There rose [1527] a secret bruit in London that the King's con-fessor, Dr. Longland, and divers other great clerks had told the King that the marriage between him and the Lady Katherine, late wife to his brother Prince Arthur, was not lawful; whereupon the King should sue a divorce, and marry the Duchess of Alençon, sister to the French king. . . . The King was offended with those tales, and sent for Sir Thomas Seymour, Mayor of the city of London, secretly charging him to see that the people ceased from such talk. . . .

The truth is that, whether this doubt was first moved by the Cardinal or by the said Longland, . . . the King was . . . determined to have the case examined, cleared, and adjudged by learning, law, and sufficient authority. The Cardinal verily was put in most blame for this scruple now cast into the King's conscience, for the hate he bare to the Emperor, because he would not grant to him the archbishopric of Toledo, for the which he was a suitor. And therefore he did not only procure the king of England to join in friendship with the French king, but also sought a divorce betwixt the King and the Queen that the King might have had in marriage the Duchess of Alençon. . . .

. . . the King . . . thus troubled in conscience . . . , to have the doubt clearly removed, he called together the best learned of the realm, which were of several opinions; wherefore he thought to know the truth by indifferent judges, lest peradventure the Spaniards and other also in favor of the Queen would say that his own subjects were not indifferent judges in this behalf. And therefore he wrote his cause to Rome, and also sent . . . to the great clerks of all christendom, to know their opinions, and desired the court of Rome to send into his realm a legate, which should be indifferent, and of a great and profound judgment, to hear the cause debated; at whose request the whole consistory of the College of Rome sent thither Laurence Campeius, a priest cardinal, a man of great wit and experience, . . . and with him was joined in commission the Cardinal of York and legate of England. . . .

The place where the cardinals should sit to hear the cause of matrimony . . . was ordained to be at the Blackfriars in London, where in the great hall was preparation made of seats, tables, and other furniture, according to such a solemn session and royal appearance. The court was platted in tables and benches in manner of a consistory, one seat raised higher for the judges to sit in. Then, as it were in the midst of the said judges, aloft above them three degrees high, was a cloth of estate hanged, with a chair royal under the same, wherein sat the King; and besides him, some distance from him sat the Queen, and under the judges' feet sat the scribes and other officers. . . .

Then before the King and the judges within the court sat the Archbishop of Canterbury, Warham, and all the other bishops. . . . The judges commanded silence whilst their commission was read, both to the court and to the people assembled. That done, the scribes commanded the crier to call the King by the name of "King Henry of England, come into the court," etc. With that the King answered and said, "Here." Then called he the Queen by the name of "Katherine, Queen of England, come into the court," etc.; who made no answer, but rose out of her chair.

And because she could not come to the King directly, for the distance severed between them, she went about by the court and came to the King, kneeling down at his feet, to whom she said in effect as followeth: "Sir" (quoth she), "I desire you to do me justice and right, and take some pity upon me, for I am a poor woman, and a stranger, born out of your dominion, having here no indifferent counsel, and less assurance of friendship. Alas, sir, what have I offended you, or what occasion of displeasure have I showed you, intending thus to put me from you after this sort? I take God to my judge, I have been to you a true and humble wife, ever conformable to your will and pleasure, that never contraried or gainsaid anything thereof, and being always contented with all things wherein you had any delight, whether little or much. Without grudge or displeasure, I loved for your sake all them whom you loved, whether they were my friends or enemies.

"I have been your wife these twenty years and more, and you have had by me divers children. If there be any just cause that you can allege against me, either of dishonesty, or matter lawful to put me from you, I am content to depart to my shame and rebuke; and if there be none, then I pray you to let me have justice at your hand. The King your father was in his time of excellent wit, and the king of Spain, my father Ferdinando, was reckoned one of the wisest princes that reigned in Spain many years before. It is not to be doubted but that they had gathered as wise counsellors unto them of every realm as to their wisdoms they thought meet, who deemed the marriage between you and me good and lawful (etc.). Wherefore, I humbly desire you to spare me, until I may know what counsel my friends in Spain will advertise me to take, and if you will not, then your pleasure be fulfilled." With that she arose up, making a low curtsy to the King, and departed from thence.

The King, being advertised that she was ready to go out of the house, commanded the crier to call her again, who called her by these words: "Katherine, Queen of England, come into the court." With that, quoth Master Griffith, "Madam, you be called again." "On, on" (quoth she), "it maketh no matter, I will not tarry; go on your ways." And thus she departed, without any further answer at that time or any other, and never would appear after in any court. The King, perceiving she was departed, said these words in effect: "Forasmuch . . . as the Queen is gone, I will in her absence declare to you all, that she hath been to me as true, as obedient, and as conformable a wife as I would wish or desire. She hath all the virtuous qualities that ought to be in a woman of her dignity, or in any other of a baser estate. She is also surely a noblewoman born: her conditions will well declare the same."

With that quoth Wolsey the Cardinal: "Sir, I most humbly require your Highness to declare before all this audience whether I have been the chief and first mover of this matter unto your Majesty or no, for I am greatly suspected herein." "My Lord Cardinal" (quoth the King),

"I can well excuse you in this matter; marry, . . . you have been rather against me in the tempting hereof than a setter forward or mover of the same. The special cause that moved me unto this matter was a certain scrupulosity that pricked my conscience, upon certain words spoken at a time when it was, by the Bishop of Bayonne, the French ambassador, who had been hither sent, upon the debating of a marriage to be concluded between our daughter, the Lady Mary, and the Duke of Orleans, second son to the king of France.

"Upon the resolution and determination whereof, he desired respite to advertise the King his master thereof, whether our daughter Mary should be legitimate in respect of this my marriage with this woman, being sometimes my brother's wife; which words, once conceived within the secret bottom of my conscience, engendered such a scrupulous doubt that my conscience was incontinently accombered, vexed, and disquieted; whereby I thought myself to be greatly in danger of God's indignation—which appeared to be (as me seemed) the rather, for that He sent us no issue male, and all such issues male as my said wife had by me died incontinent after they came into the world, so that I doubted the great displeasure of God in that behalf.

"Thus my conscience being tossed in the waves of a scrupulous mind, and partly in despair to have any other issue than I had already by this lady now my wife, it behooved me further to consider the state of this realm and the danger it stood in for lack of a prince to succeed me, I thought it good in release of the weighty burden of my weak conscience, and also the quiet estate of this worthy realm, to attempt the law therein, whether I may lawfully take another wife . . . by whom God may send me more issue, . . . not for any displeasure or misliking of the Queen's person and age, with whom I would be as well contented to continue, if our marriage may stand with the laws of God, as with any woman alive.

"In this point consisteth all this doubt that we go about now to try, by the learning, wisdom, and judgment of you our prelates and pastors . . . , to whose conscience and learning I have committed the charge and judgment. . . . After that I perceived my conscience so doubtful, I moved it in confession to you, my Lord of Lincoln, then ghostly father. And forsomuch as then you yourself were in some doubt, you moved me to ask the counsel of all these my lords; whereupon I moved you, my Lord of Canterbury, first to have your license . . . to put this matter in question. And so I did of all you, my lords; to which you granted, under your seals, here to be showed." "That is truth," quoth the Archbishop of Canterbury. After that the King rose up, and the court was adjourned until another day.

Here is to be noted that the Queen, in presence of the whole court, most grievously accused the Cardinal of untruth, deceit, wickedness, and malice, which had sown dissension betwixt her and the King her husband; and therefore openly protested that she did utterly abhor, refuse, and forsake such a judge, as was not only a most malicious enemy to her, but also a manifest adversary to all right and justice; and therewith did she appeal unto the Pope, committing her whole cause to be judged of him. But notwithstanding this appeal, the legates sat weekly, . . . and still they assayed if they could by any means procure the Queen to call back her appeal, which she utterly refused to do. The King would gladly have had an end in the matter, but when the legates drave time and determined upon no certain point, he conceived a suspicion, that this was done of purpose, that their doings might draw to none effect or conclusion. . . .

[II.i] And thus this court passed from . . . day to day, till at certain of their sessions the King sent the two cardinals to the Queen . . . to persuade with her by their wisdoms and to advise her to surrender the whole matter into the King's hands by her own consent and will; which should be much better to her honor than to stand to the trial of law, and thereby to be condemned. . . .

. . . the gentleman usher advertised the Queen that the cardinals were come to speak with her. With that she rose up, and with a skein of white thread about her neck, came into her chamber of presence, where the cardinals were attending. At whose coming, quoth she, "What is your pleasure with me?" "If it please your Grace" (quoth Cardinal Wolsey), "to go into your privy chamber, we will show you the cause of our coming." "My lord" (quoth she), "if ye have anything to say, speak it openly before all these folk, for I fear nothing that ye can say against me, but that I would all the world should hear and see it, and therefore speak your mind." Then began the Cardinal to speak to her in Latin. "Nay, good my lord" (quoth she), "speak to me in English."

"Forsooth" (quoth the Cardinal), "good madam, if it please you, we come both to know your mind how you are disposed to do in this matter between the King and you, and also to declare secretly our opinions and counsel unto you; which we do only for very zeal and obedience we bear unto your Grace." "My lord" (quoth she), "I thank you for your good will, but to make you answer in your request I cannot so suddenly, for I was set among my maids at work, thinking full little of any such matter, wherein there needeth a longer deliberation and a better head than mine to make answer; for I need counsel in this case which toucheth me so near, and for any counsel or friendship that I can find in England, they are not for my profit. What think you, my lords, will any Englishman counsel me, or be friend to me against the King's pleasure that is his subject? Nay, forsooth. And as for my council in whom I will put my trust, they be not here, they be in Spain in my own country.

"And, my lords, I am a poor woman, lacking wit, to answer to any such noble persons of wisdom as you be, in so weighty a matter. Therefore I pray you be good to me, poor woman, destitute of friends here in a foreign region, and your counsel also I will be glad to hear." And therewith she took the Cardinal by the hand, and led him into her privy chamber with the other cardinal, where they tarried a season talking with the Queen. . . .

[II.iv. 230–37] . . . the King's counsel at the bar called

for judgment. . . . Quoth Cardinal Campeius: "I . . . will adjourn this court for this time, according to the order of the court of Rome." And with that the court was dissolved. . . . This protracting of the conclusion of the matter, King Henry took very displeasantly. . . .

[III.ii] Whilst these things were thus in hand, the Cardinal of York was advised that the King had set his affection upon a young gentlewoman named Anne, the daughter of Sir Thomas Bullen, Viscount Rochford, which did wait upon the Queen. This was a great grief unto the Cardinal, as he that perceived aforehand that the King would marry the said gentlewoman if the divorce took place; wherefore he began with all diligence to disappoint that match, which by reason of the misliking that he had to the woman, he judged ought to be avoided more than present death. . . . The Cardinal required the Pope by letters and secret messengers that in any wise he should defer the judgment of the divorce till he might frame the King's mind to his purpose.

Howbeit he went about nothing so secretly but that the same came to the King's knowledge, who took so high displeasure with such his cloaked dissimulation that he determined to abase his degree. . . . When the nobles of the realm perceived the Cardinal to be in displeasure, they began to accuse him of such offenses as they knew might be proved against him, and thereof they made a book containing certain articles, to which divers of the King's council set their hands. The King, understanding more plainly by those articles the great pride, presumption, and covetousness of the Cardinal, was sore moved against him; but yet kept his purpose secret for a while. . . .

In the meantime the King, being informed that all those things that the Cardinal had done by his power legantine within this realm were in the case of the præmunire and provision, caused his attorney, Christopher Hales, to sue out a writ of præmunire against him. . . . And further . . . the King sent the two dukes of Norfolk and Suffolk to the Cardinal's place at Westminster, who . . . , finding the Cardinal there, they declared that the King's pleasure was that he should surrender up the Great Seal into their hands, and to depart simply unto Asher, which was an house situate nigh unto Hampton Court, belonging to the bishopric of Winchester. The Cardinal demanded of them their commission that gave them such authority; who answered again, that they were sufficient commissioners and had authority to do no less by the King's mouth. Notwithstanding, he would in no wise agree in that behalf without further knowledge of their authority, saying that the Great Seal was delivered him by the King's person, to enjoy the ministration thereof, with the room of the chancellor for the term of his life, whereof for his surety he had the King's letters patents.

This matter was greatly debated between them . . . insomuch that the dukes were fain to depart again without their purpose . . . ; but the next day they returned again, bringing with them the King's letters. Then the Cardinal delivered unto them the Great Seal. . . . Then the Cardinal called all his officers before him and took accompt of them for all such stuff whereof they had charge. And in his gallery were set divers tables whereupon lay a great number of goodly rich stuff. . . .

There was laid, on every table, books reporting the contents of the same, and so was there inventories of all things in order against the King's coming. . . . Then had he two chambers adjoining to the gallery, . . . wherein were set up two broad and long tables upon trestles, whereupon was set such a number of plate of all sorts as was almost incredible. . . .

After this, in the King's Bench his matter for the præmunire being called upon, two attorneys, which he had authorized by his warrant . . . , confessed the action, and so had judgment to forfeit all his lands, tenements, goods, and chattels, and to be out of the King's protection. . . .

During this Parliament was brought down to the Commons the book of articles, which the Lords had put to the King against the Cardinal, the chief whereof were these:

1. First, that he without the King's assent had procured to be a legate, by reason whereof he took away the right of all bishops and spiritual persons.

2. Item, in all writings which he wrote to Rome or any other foreign prince, he wrote *Ego et rex meus,* I and my King; as who would say that the King were his servant.

3. Item, that he hath slandered the Church of England in the court of Rome. . . .

4. Item, he without the King's assent carried the King's Greal Seal with him into Flanders, when he was sent ambassador to the Emperor.

5. Item, he without the King's assent sent a commission to Sir Gregory de Cassado, Kt., to conclude a league between the King and the Duke of Ferrar, without the King's knowledge.

6. Item, that he, having the French pox, presumed to come and breathe on the King.

7. Item, that he caused the Cardinal's hat to be put on the King's coin.

8. Item, that he would not suffer the King's clerk of the market to sit at St. Albans.

9. Item, that he had sent innumerable substance to Rome, for the obtaining of his dignities, to the great impoverishment of the realm. . . .

[II.iv.108–17; III.ii.455–57; V.ii.5–68] [After being permitted to journey to York, the Cardinal was arrested for high treason at Cawood by the Earl of Northumberland. On the way south the Cardinal "waxed very sick."] The next day he rode to Nottingham and there lodged that night more sick; and the next day he rode to Leicester Abbey, and by the way waxed so sick that he was almost fallen from his mule; so that it was night before he came to the abbey of Leicester, where at his coming in at the gates, the abbot with all his convent met him with divers torches' light, whom they honorably received and welcomed.

To whom the Cardinal said: "Father abbot, I am come hither to lay my bones among you," . . . and as soon as he was in his chamber he went to bed. This was on the

Saturday at night, and then increased he sicker and sicker, until Monday, that all men thought he would have died. So on Tuesday . . . Master Kingston came to him and bade him good morrow. . . .

"Well, well, Master Kingston" (quoth the Cardinal), "I see the matter how it is framed; but if I had served God as diligently as I have done the King, he would not have given me over in my gray hairs. . . ."

Then they did put him in remembrance of Christ His passion, . . . and incontinent the clock struck eight, and then he gave up the ghost and departed this present life; which caused some to call to remembrance how he said the day before that at eight of the clock they should lose their master.

Here is the end and fall of pride and arrogancy of men exalted by fortune to dignity: for in his time he was the haughtiest man in all his proceedings alive, having more respect to the honor of his person than he had to his spiritual profession, wherein should be showed all meekness, humility, and charity. . . .

This Cardinal (as Edmund Campian in his history of Ireland describeth him) was a man undoubtedly born to honor: "I think" (saith he), "some prince's bastard, no butcher's son; exceeding wise, fair spoken, high minded; full of revenge; vicious of his body; lofty to his enemies, were they never so big; to those that accepted and sought his friendship, wonderful courteous; a ripe schoolman; thrall to affections; brought abed with flattery; insatiable to get, and more princely in bestowing, as appeareth by his two colleges at Ipswich and Oxenford, the one overthrown with his fall, the other unfinished, and yet as it lieth for an house of students, considering all the appurtenances, incomparable through Christendom. . . . [He was] never happy till this his overthrow; wherein he showed such moderation and ended so perfectly that the hour of his death did him more honor than all the pomp of his life past.". . .

This Thomas Wolsey was a poor man's son of Ipswich, . . . and being but a child, very apt to be learned. . . .

[II.iv.Entry] [The Cardinal's pomp and ceremony are

described.] Before him was borne first the Broad Seal of England and his cardinal's hat by a lord or some gentleman of worship, right solemnly, and as soon as he was once entered into his chamber of presence his two great crosses were there attending to be borne before him. Then cried the gentlemen ushers, going before him bareheaded, and said: "On before, my lords and masters, on before; make way for my lord's Grace." Thus went he down through the hall with a Sergeant of Arms before him, bearing a great mace of silver, and two gentlemen carrying two great pillars of silver. . . .

[I.iv] Thus in great honor, triumph, and glory, he reigned a long season. . . . And when it pleased the King for his recreation to repair to the Cardinal's house . . . there wanted no preparations or furniture. . . .

On a time the King came suddenly thither in a masque with a dozen masquers all in garments like shepherds. . . . And before his entering into the hall, he came by water to the water gate without any noise, where were laid divers chambers and guns charged with shot, and at his landing they were shot off. . . . It made all the noblemen, gentlemen, ladies, and gentlewomen to muse what it should mean, coming so suddenly, they sitting quiet at a solemn banquet. . . .

First ye shall understand that the tables were set in the chamber of presence . . . and the Lord Cardinal sitting under the cloth of estate, there having all his service alone; and then was there set a lady with a nobleman, or a gentleman and a gentlewoman, throughout all the tables in the chamber on the one side, which were made and joined as it were but one table, all which order and device was done by the Lord Sands, then Lord Chamberlain to the King, and by Sir Henry Guildford, comptroller of the King's Majesty's house. Then immediately after, the Great Chamberlain and the said comptroller, sent to look what it should mean (as though they knew nothing of the matter), who looking out of the windows into the Thames, returned again and showed him, that it seemed they were noblemen and strangers that arrived at his bridge, coming as ambassadors from some foreign prince.

With that (quoth the Cardinal), "I desire you, because you can speak French, to take the pains to go into the hall, there to receive them according to their estates, and to conduct them into this chamber, where they shall see us and all these noble personages being merry at our banquet, desiring them to sit down with us and to take part of our fare." Then . . . they received them . . . and conveyed them up into the chamber. . . . At their entering into the chamber two and two together, they went directly before the Cardinal, where he sate, and saluted him reverently.

To whom the Lord Chamberlain, for them, said: "Sir, forasmuch as they be strangers and cannot speak English, they have desired me to declare unto you that they having understanding of this your triumphant banquet, where was assembled such a number of excellent dames, they could do no less under support of your Grace but to repair hither to view as well their incomparable beauty, . . . and . . . to dance with them; and sir, they require of your Grace license to accomplish the said cause of their coming." To whom the Cardinal said he was very well content they should so do. Then went the masquers and first saluted all the dames. . . .

Then spake the Lord Chamberlain to them in French, and they rounding [whispering to] him in the ear, the Lord Chamberlain said to my Lord Cardinal: "Sir, . . . they confess that among them there is such a noble personage, whom, if your Grace can appoint him out from the rest, he is content to disclose himself and to accept your place." With that, the Cardinal taking good advisement among them, at the last quoth he, "Meseemeth the gentleman with the black beard should be even he"; and with that he arose out of his chair, and offered the same to the gentleman in the black beard with his cap in his hand. The person to whom he offered the chair was Sir Edward Nevill. . . .

The King, perceiving the Cardinal so deceived, could not forbear laughing, but pulled down his visor and Master Nevill's also. . . . The Cardinal eftsoons desired his Highness to take the place of estate; to whom the

King answered that he would go first and shift his apparel, and so departed into my Lord Cardinal's chamber and there new appareled him. . . .

Then the King took his seat under the cloth of estate. . . . Thus passed they forth the night with banqueting, dancing, and other triumphs, to the great comfort of the King and pleasant regard of the nobility there assembled. . . .

[IV.ii.33–44] This Cardinal . . . was of a great stomach, for he compted himself equal with princes and by crafty suggestion got into his hands innumerable treasure. He forced little on simony, and was not pitiful, and stood affectionate in his own opinion. In open presence he would lie and say untruth, and was double both in speech and meaning; he would promise much and perform little. He was vicious of his body and gave the clergy evil example. . . .

[II.iii.60–65] On the first of September [1532] . . . the King, being come to Windsor, created the Lady Anne Boleyn Marchioness of Pembroke, and gave to her one thousand pounds land by the year. . . .

[III.ii.41–42, 67–71, 400–06; IV.i.22–33, 108–12] [The King journeyed to France, 1532.] And herewith upon his return, he married privily the Lady Anne Boleyn the same day, being the fourteenth day of November . . . ; which marriage was kept so secret that very few knew it till Easter next ensuing, when it was perceived that she was with child. . . .

It was also enacted the same time [1533] that Queen Katherine should no more be called Queen, but Princess Dowager, as the widow of Prince Arthur. In the season of the last summer died William Warham, Archbishop of Canterbury, and then was named to that see Thomas Cranmer, the King's chaplain, a man of good learning and of a virtuous life, which lately before had been ambassador from the King to the Pope.

After that the King perceived his new wife to be with child, he caused all officers necessary to be appointed to her, and so on Easter Even she went to her closet openly as Queen; and then the King appointed the day of her

coronation to be kept on Whitsunday next following. . . .
The assessment of the fine was appointed to Thomas
Cromwell, Master of the King's Jewel House and council-
lor to the King, a man newly received into high favor. . . .

. . . the Lady Katherine Dowager (for so was she
then called) . . . persisted still in her former opinion and
would revoke by no means her appeal to the court of
Rome; whereupon the Archbishop of Canterbury, accompanied with the bishops of London, Winchester, Bath,
Lincoln, and divers other learned men in great number,
rode to Dunstable, which is six miles from Ampthill,
where the Princess Dowager lay, and there . . . she was
cited to appear before the said Archbishop in cause of
matrimony . . . and . . . she appeared not but made
default, and so she was called peremptory every day
fifteen days together, and at the last, for lack of appearance, by the assent of all the learned men there present,
she was divorced from the King, and the marriage declared to be void and of none effect. . . .

[IV.i.36–94] [The coronation is described.] First went
gentlemen, then esquires, then knights, then the aldermen . . . , after them the judges in their mantles of scarlet
and coifs. Then followed the Knights of the Bath. . . .
After them came the Lord Chancellor in a robe of scarlet
open before. . . . After him came the King's chapel and
the monks solemnly singing with procession. Then came
abbots and bishops mitered. . . . Then after them went
the Mayor of London, with his mace and garter, in his
coat of arms. Then went the Marquess Dorset in a robe
of estate which bare the scepter of gold, and the Earl of
Arundell, which bare the rod of ivory with the dove both
together.

Then went alone the Earl of Oxford . . . which bare
the crown. After him went the Duke of Suffolk in his
robe of estate, also for that day being High Steward of
England, having a long white rod in his hand, and the
Lord William Howard [Norfolk] with the rod of the
marshalship, and every Knight of the Garter had on his
collar of the order. Then proceeded forth the Queen in a
surcoat and robe of purple velvet furred with ermine, in

her hair, coif, and circlet . . . , and over her was borne
the canopy by four of the five ports, all crimson with
points of blue and red hanging on their sleeves; and the
bishops of London and Winchester bare up the laps of
the Queen's robe. The Queen's train, which was very
long, was borne by the old Duchess of Norfolk. After
her followed ladies, being lords' wives, which had sur-
coats of scarlet. . . .

When she was thus brought to the high place made in
the midst of the church, between the choir and the high
altar, she was set in a rich chair. And after that she had
rested a while, she descended down to the high altar and
there prostrate herself while the Archbishop of Canterbury said certain collects. Then she rose, and the Bishop
anointed her on the head and on the breast, and then
she was led up again, where, after divers orisons said, the
Archbishop set the crown of St. Edward on her head
and then delivered her the scepter of gold in her right
hand and the rod of ivory with the dove in the left hand,
and then all the choir sung "Te Deum," etc. . . .

Now, in the mean season, every duchess had put on
their bonnets a coronal of gold wrought with flowers, and
every marquess put on a demicoronal of gold, every
countess a plain circlet of gold without flowers, and every
King of Arms put on a crown of copper and gilt, all
which were worn till night. When the Queen had a little
reposed her, the company returned in the same order
that they set forth. . . .

[V.i.158–70; V.v.Entry] The seventh of September . . .
the Queen was delivered of a fair young lady, on which
day the Duke of Norfolk came home to the christening,
which was appointed on the Wednesday next following. . . . The godfather at the font was the Lord Archbishop of Canterbury; the godmothers, the old Duchess
of Norfolk and the old Marchioness Dorset, widow. . . .
The child was named Elizabeth. . . . [A description of
the christening follows.]

When the ceremonies and christening were ended,
Garter chief King of Arms cried aloud, "God of His
infinite goodness send prosperous life and long to the high

and mighty Princess of England, Elizabeth," and then the trumpets blew. Then the Archbishop of Canterbury gave to the Princess a standing cup of gold. The Duchess of Norfolk gave to her a standing cup of gold, fretted with pearl. The Marchioness of Dorset gave three gilt bowls, pounced with a cover. . . . Then they set forwards, the trumpets going before. . . .

[IV.ii.105–54] The Princess Dowager, lying at Kimbolton, fell into her last sickness, whereof the King, being advertised, appointed the Emperor's ambassador, . . . Eustachius Caputius, to go to visit her and to do his commendations to her and will her to be of good comfort. The ambassador with all diligence did his duty therein, comforting her the best he might; but she within six days after, perceiving herself to wax very weak and feeble and to feel death approaching at hand, caused one of her gentlewomen to write a letter to the King, commending to him her daughter and his, beseeching him to stand good father unto her; and further desired him to have some consideration of her gentlewomen that had served her, and to see them bestowed in marriage; further, that it would please him to appoint that her servants might have their due wages and a year's wages beside. This, in effect, was all that she requested, and so immediately hereupon she departed this life. . . .

JOHN FOXE

from *Acts and Monuments of Martyrs*
(1597 edition)

[V.iii.175–77] . . . it came into a common proverb: Do unto my lord of Canterbury displeasure or a shrewd turn, and then you may be sure to have him your friend whiles he liveth. . . .

[V.i; V.ii] . . . certain of the council . . . by the enticement and provocation of his ancient enemy the Bishop of Winchester, and other of the same sect, attempted the King against him, declaring plainly that the realm was so infected with heresies and heretics that it was dangerous to his Highness farther to permit it unreformed, lest . . . such contention should arise . . . among his subjects that thereby might spring horrible commotions and uproars, like as in some parts of Germany it did, not long ago; the enormity whereof they could not impute to any so much as to the Archbishop of Canterbury, who, by his own preaching and his chaplains', had filled the whole realm full of divers pernicious heresies. The King would needs know his accusers. They answered that forasmuch as he was a councillor no man durst take upon him to accuse him, but if it would please his Highness to commit him to the Tower for a time, there would be accusations and proofs enough against him.

The King, perceiving their importunate suit against the Archbishop (but yet not meaning to have him wronged . . .), granted unto them that they should the next day commit him to the Tower for his trial. When night came, the King sent Sir Anthony Denny, about midnight, to Lambeth to the Archbishop, willing him forthwith to resort unto him at the court. . . . The Archbishop . . . coming into the gallery where the King walked, and tarried for him, his Highness said: "Ah, my lord of Canterbury, I can tell you news. For divers weighty considerations it is determined by me, and the council, that you tomorrow at nine of the clock shall be committed to the Tower, for that you and your chaplains . . . have taught and preached and thereby sown within the realm such a number of execrable heresies, that it is feared, the whole realm being infected with them, no small contention and commotions will rise thereby amongst my subjects, as of late days the like was in divers parts of Germany, and therefore the council have requested me, for the trial of the matter, to suffer them to commit you to the Tower, or else no man dare come forth as witness in these matters, you being a councillor."

When the King had said his mind, the Archbishop kneeled down and said: "I am content if it please your Grace, with all my heart, to go thither at your Highness' commandment, and I most humbly thank your Majesty that I may come to my trial, for there be that have many ways slandered me, and now this way I hope to try myself not worthy of such report."

The King perceiving the man's uprightness, joined with such simplicity, said: "Oh, lord, what manner a man be you? What simplicity is in you? I had thought that you would rather have sued to us to have taken the pains to have heard you and your accusers together for your trial, without any such indurance. Do not you know what state you be in with the whole world, and how many great enemies you have? Do you not consider what an easy thing it is to procure three or four false knaves to witness against you? Think you to have better luck that way than your master Christ had? I see by it, you will run headlong to your undoing if I would suffer you. Your enemies shall not so prevail against you, for I have otherwise devised with myself to keep you out of their hands. Yet notwithstanding, tomorrow when the council shall sit and send for you, resort unto them, and if in charging you with this matter they do commit you to the Tower, require of them ... that you may have your accusers brought before them without any further indurance, and use for yourself as good persuasions that way as you may devise, and if no entreaty or reasonable request will serve, then deliver unto them this my ring ... and say unto them, 'If there be no remedy, my lords, but that I must needs go to the Tower, then I revoke my cause from you, and appeal to the King's own person by this token unto you all,' for ... so soon as they shall see this my ring, they know it so well that they shall understand that I have resumed the whole cause into mine own hands. ..."

The Archbishop, perceiving the King's benignity so much to him wards, had much ado to forbear tears. "Well," said the King, "go your ways, my lord, and do as I have bidden you." My lord, humbling himself with thanks, took his leave of the King's Highness for that night.

On the morrow about nine of the clock before noon, the council sent a gentleman usher for the Archbishop, who, when he came to the council-chamber door, could not be let in, but of purpose (as it seemed) was compelled there to wait among the pages, lackies, and servingmen all alone. Dr. Butts, the King's physician, resorting that way and espying how my lord of Canterbury was handled, went to the King's Highness and said: "My lord of Canterbury, if it please your Grace, is well promoted; for now he is become a lackey or a servingman, for yonder he standeth this half hour at the council-chamber door amongst them." "It is not so" (quoth the King), "I trow, nor the council hath not so little discretion as to use the metropolitan of the realm in that sort, specially being one of their own number. But let them alone, ... and we shall hear more soon."

Anon the Archbishop was called into the council-chamber, to whom was alleged as before is rehearsed. The Archbishop answered in like sort as the King had advised him; and in the end when he perceived that no manner of persuasion or entreaty could serve, he delivered them the King's ring, revoking his cause into the King's hands. The whole council being thereat somewhat amazed, the Earl of Bedford with a loud voice, confirming his words with a solemn oath, said: "When you first began the matter, my lords, I told you what would come of it. Do you think that the King will suffer this man's finger to ache? Much more, I warrant you, will he defend his life against brabling varlets. You do but cumber yourselves to hear tales and fables against him." And so incontinently upon the receipt of the King's token, they all rose and carried to the King his ring, surrendering that matter, as the order and use was, into his own hands.

When they were all come to the King's presence, his Highness, with a severe countenance, said unto them: "Ah, my lords, I thought I had had wiser men of my council than now I find you. What discretion was this in you, thus to make the Primate of the realm, and one of you in office, to wait at the council-chamber door amongst servingmen? You might have considered that he was a councillor as well as you, and you had no such commission of me so to handle him. I was content that you should try him as a councillor and not as a mean subject. But now I well perceive that things be done against him maliciously, and if some of you might have had your minds, you would have tried him to the uttermost. But I do you all to wit, and protest, that if a prince may be beholding unto his subject" (and so, solemnly laying his hand upon his breast, said), "by the faith I owe to God, I take this man here, my lord of Canterbury, to be of all other a most faithful subject unto us, and one to whom we are much beholding." ... And, with that, one or two of the chiefest of the council, making their excuse, declared that in re-questing his indurance, it was rather meant for his trial, and his purgation against the common fame and slander of the world, than for any malice conceived against him.

"Well, well, my lords" (quoth the King), "take him and well use him, as he is worthy to be, and make no more ado." And with that every man caught him by the hand, and made fair weather of altogethers, which might easily be done with that man.

Commentaries

WILLIAM HAZLITT

from *Characters of Shakespear's Plays*

This play contains little action or violence of passion, yet it has considerable interest of a more mild and thoughtful cast, and some of the most striking passages in the author's works. The character of Queen Katherine is the most perfect delineation of matronly dignity, sweetness, and resignation, that can be conceived. Her appeals to the protection of the king, her remonstrances to the cardinals, her conversations with her women, show a noble and generous spirit accompanied with the utmost gentleness of nature. What can be more affecting than her answer to Campeius and Wolsey, who come to visit her as pretended friends.

> ———"Nay, forsooth, my friends,
> They that must weigh out my afflictions,

From *Characters of Shakespear's Plays* by William Hazlitt. 2nd ed. London: Taylor & Hessey, 1818.

> They that my trust must grow to, live not here;
> They are, as all my comforts are, far hence,
> In mine own country, lords."

Dr. Johnson observes of this play, that "the meek sorrows and virtuous distress of Katherine have furnished some scenes, which may be justly numbered among the greatest efforts of tragedy. But the genius of Shakespear comes in and goes out with Katherine. Every other part may be easily conceived and easily written." This is easily said; but with all due deference to so great a reputed authority as that of Johnson, it is not true. For instance, the scene of Buckingham led to execution is one of the most affecting and natural in Shakespear, and one to which there is hardly an approach in any other author. Again, the character of Wolsey, the description of his pride and of his fall, are inimitable, and have, besides their gorgeousness of effect, a pathos, which only the genius of Shakespear could lend to the distresses of a proud, bad man, like Wolsey. There is a sort of child-like simplicity in the very helplessness of his situation, arising from the recollection of his past overbearing ambition. After the cutting sarcasms of his enemies on his disgrace, against which he bears up with a spirit conscious of his own superiority, he breaks out into that fine apostrophe—

> "Farewell, a long farewell, to all my greatness!
> This is the state of man; today he puts forth
> The tender leaves of hope, tomorrow blossoms,
> And bears his blushing honors thick upon him;
> The third day comes a frost, a killing frost;
> And—when he thinks, good easy man, full surely
> His greatness is a ripening—nips his root,
> And then he falls, as I do. I have ventur'd,
> Like little wanton boys that swim on bladders,
> These many summers in a sea of glory;
> But far beyond my depth: my high-blown pride
> At length broke under me; and now has left me,
> Weary and old with service, to the mercy
> Of a rude stream, that must for ever hide me.

Vain pomp and glory of the world, I hate ye!
I feel my heart new open'd: O how wretched
Is that poor man, that hangs on princes' favors!
There is betwixt that smile we would aspire to,
That sweet aspect of princes, and our ruin,
More pangs and fears than war and women have;
And when he falls, he falls like Lucifer,
Never to hope again!"—

There is in this passage, as well as in the well-known dialogue with Cromwell which follows, something which stretches beyond commonplace; nor is the account which Griffiths gives of Wolsey's death less Shakespearian; and the candor with which Queen Katherine listens to the praise of "him whom of all men living she hated most" adds the last graceful finishing to her character.

Among other images of great individual beauty might be mentioned the description of the effect of Ann Boleyn's presenting herself to the crowd at her coronation.

————"While her grace sat down
To rest awhile, some half an hour or so,
In a rich chair of state, opposing freely
The beauty of her person to the people.
Believe me, sir, she is the goodliest woman
That ever lay by man. Which when the people
Had the full view of, *such a noise arose*
As the shrouds make at sea in a stiff tempest,
As loud and to as many tunes."

The character of Henry VIII is drawn with great truth and spirit. It is like a very disagreeable portrait, sketched by the hand of a master. His gross appearance, his blustering demeanor, his vulgarity, his arrogance, his sensuality, his cruelty, his hypocrisy, his want of common decency and common humanity, are marked in strong lines. His traditional peculiarities of expression complete the reality of the picture. The authoritative expletive, "Ha!" with which he intimates his indignation or surprise, has an effect like the first startling sound that breaks from a thundercloud. He is of all the monarchs in our history the most disgusting: for he unites in himself all the vices of barbarism and refinement, without their virtues. Other kings before him (such as Richard III) were tyrants and murderers out of ambition or necessity: they gained or established unjust power by violent means: they destroyed their enemies, or those who barred their access to the throne or made its tenure insecure. But Henry VIII's power is most fatal to those whom he loves: he is cruel and remorseless to pamper his luxurious appetites: bloody and voluptuous; an amorous murderer; an uxorious debauchee. His hardened insensibility to the feelings of others is strengthened by the most profligate self-indulgence. The religious hypocrisy, under which he masks his cruelty and his lust, is admirably displayed in the speech in which he describes the first misgivings of his conscience and its increasing throes and terrors, which have induced him to divorce his queen. The only thing in his favor in this play is his treatment of Cranmer: there is also another circumstance in his favor, which is his patronage of Hans Holbein.—It has been said of Shakespear—"No maid could live near such a man." It might with as good reason be said—"No king could live near such a man." His eye would have penetrated through the pomp of circumstance and the veil of opinion. As it is, he has represented such persons to the life—his plays are in this respect the glass of history—he has done them the same justice as if he had been a privy counsellor all his life, and in each successive reign. Kings ought never to be seen upon the stage. In the abstract, they are very disagreeable characters: it is only while living that they are "the best of kings." It is their power, their splendor, it is the apprehension of the personal consequences of their favor or their hatred that dazzles the imagination and suspends the judgment of their favorites or their vassals; but death cancels the bond of allegiance and of interest; and seen *as they were,* their power and their pretensions look monstrous and ridiculous. The charge brought against modern philosophy as inimical to loyalty is unjust, because it might as well be brought against other things. No reader of history can be a lover of kings. We have often wondered that Henry VIII as he is drawn by Shakespear, and as we have seen him represented in all the bloated deformity of mind and person, is not hooted from the English stage.

CAROLINE F. E. SPURGEON

from *Shakespeare's Imagery*

In *Henry VIII,* so far removed in treatment and spirit
from *King John,* the dominating image, curiously enough,
is again the body and bodily action . . . , but used in an
entirely different way and at a different angle from that in
the earlier play. The continuous picture or symbol in the
poet's mind is not so much a person displaying certain
emotions and characteristics, as a mere physical body in
endlessly varied action. Thus I find only four "personifi-
cations" in the play, whereas in *King John* I count no less
than forty.

In a play like *Henry VIII,* a large part of which it has
been generally decided on good critical grounds is not
written by Shakespeare, the question which immediately
presents itself is whether there is any evidence or not
in the imagery that one mind has functioned throughout.
For our present purpose, however, I suggest we leave
this question aside, and look at the way the running
symbol works out as a whole.

There are three aspects of the picture of a body in
the mind of the writer of the play: the whole body and
its limbs; the various parts, tongue, mouth and so on;
and—much the most constant—bodily action of almost
every kind: walking, stepping, marching, running and
leaping; crawling, hobbling, falling, carrying, climbing

From *Shakespeare's Imagery and What It Tells Us* by Caroline F. E.
Spurgeon. London: Cambridge University Press, 1935. Reprinted by permission of the publisher.

and perspiring; swimming, diving, flinging and peeping; crushing, strangling, shaking, trembling, sleeping, stirring, and—especially and repeatedly—the picture of the body or back bent and weighed down under a heavy burden. Except for this last, I see no special symbolic reason for the lavish use of this image, other than the fact that it is a favorite one with Shakespeare, especially the aspect of bodily movement, and we find it in the imagery from various points of view in *King Lear, Hamlet, Coriolanus, King John,* and in a lesser degree, in *Henry V* and *Troilus and Cressida.*

The opening scene—a vivid description of the tourney on the Field of the Cloth of Gold when Henry and Francis met—with its picture of bodily pomp and action, may possibly have started the image in the poet's mind, as it did in Buckingham's, when after listening to Norfolk's glowing words he asks,

> Who did guide,
> I mean, who set the body and the limbs
> Of this great sport together . . . ?   (I.i.45)

Norfolk, trying to restrain Buckingham's anger with the cardinal, says,

> Stay, my lord,
> . . . to climb steep hills
> Requires slow pace at first . . .   (I.i.129)
> . . . . .

> Be advised;
> . . . . . . we may outrun,
> By violent swiftness, that which we run at,
> And lose by over-running;

and the utter uselessness of the treaty which was the avowed object of the costly Cloth of Gold meeting is brought home by the amazingly vivid picture of a support or means of walking offered to the human body when no longer capable of any movement at all: the articles were ratified, says Buckingham, "to as much end as give a crutch to the dead" (I.i.171). At the end of the scene the original image returns, and the plot against the king is thought of as a body, so that when the nobles are arrested Buckingham exclaims,

> These are the limbs o' the plot: no more, I hope.
> (I.i.220)

We note as we read that many of the most vivid images in the play are those of movements of the body, such as Norfolk's description (II.ii.26) of Wolsey diving into the king's soul, and there scattering dangers and doubts, Cranmer, crawling into the king's favor and strangling his language in tears (V.i.156), Anne's ejaculation about Katharine's deposition, and her divorce from the majesty and pomp of sovereignty, and Katharine's

> sufferance panging
> As soul and body's severing.   (II.iii.15)

Wolsey thinks constantly in terms of body movement: among his images are those of a soldier marching in step with a "file" (I.ii.42), a man scratched and torn by pressing through a thorny wood (I.ii.75), or set on by thieves, bound, robbed and unloosed (II.iv.146); and in his last great speeches, which, in spite of falling rhythm, I incline to believe are Shakespeare's, he speaks of having *trod* the ways of glory (III.ii.435), sees Cromwell *carrying* peace in his right hand (445), urges him to *fling away* ambition (440), and pictures himself successively as a rash *swimmer* venturing far beyond his depth with the meretricious aid of a bladder (III.ii.358–61), a man *falling* headlong from a great height like a meteor (226) or like Lucifer (371), and finally, standing bare and *naked* at the mercy of his enemies (457).

The image of the back bent under the load recurs five times, and is obviously and suitably symbolic of Wolsey's state, as well as of the heavy taxation. Wolsey complains that the question of the divorce was "the weight that pulled him down" (III.ii.407), and after his dismissal, sees himself as a man with an unbearable burden suddenly lifted off him, assuring Cromwell that he thanks the king, who has cured him, "and from these shoulders" taken "a load would sink a navy,"

> a burden
> Too heavy for a man that hopes for heaven!
>
> (III.ii.384)

The idea of a man falling from a great height is constant in the case of both Wolsey and Cranmer; and the remonstrances made with their accusers are in each case exactly alike:

> Press not a falling man too far; . . .
>
> (III. ii. 333)

. . . .

> 'tis a cruelty
> To load a falling man.
>
> (V.iii.76)

The queen draws on the same range of bodily similes. She speaks of unmannerly language "which breaks the sides of loyalty," "bold mouths" and "tongues" spitting their duties out, and her description (II.iv.111–15) of the great cardinal, with the king's aid going swiftly and easily over the shallow steps until mounted at the top of the staircase of fame, is extraordinarily vivid.

The king also uses it with great force when relating his mental and emotional suffering and the self questioning that followed on hearing the French ambassador demand a "respite" [an adjournment] in order to determine whether the Princess Mary were legitimate, thus raising the whole question of the divorce.

He draws a picture of the word "respite" and its effect on him as of a rough and hasty intruder rushing noisily into a quiet and guarded place, shaking and splitting it, forcing a way in so ruthlessly that with him throng in also from outside many other unbidden beings, pressing and pushing, dazed and puzzled with the commotion and the place wherein they find themselves. "This respite," he declares,

                          shook
The bosom of my conscience, enter'd me,
Yea, with a splitting power, and made to tremble
The region of my breast; which forced such way
That many mazed considerings did throng
And press'd in with this caution.   (II.iv.181)

A little later, as he tells the court how he sought counsel
from his prelates, he, like Wolsey, pictures himself as a
man almost unbearably burdened, groaning and sweating
under his load, when he turns to the bishop with the
query,

            my lord of Lincoln; you remember
How under my oppression I did reek,
When I first moved you.   (II.iv.207)

When we trace out in detail this series of images, we
recognize that it is a good example of Shakespeare's
peculiar habit of seeing emotional or mental situations
throughout a play in a repeatedly recurring physical picture, in what might more correctly indeed be called a
"moving picture"; because having once, as here, visualized
the human body in action, he sees it continuously, like
Wolsey's "strange postures" in every form of physical
activity.

I must not, however, here be led into the question of
authorship, beyond stating that the imagery of *Henry VIII*
distinctly goes to prove that in addition to the generally
accepted Shakespearian scenes (I.i and II.ii, iii, and iv,
the early part of III.ii and V.i), the whole of III.ii and
V.iii are also his, and that he at least gave some touches
to II.ii.[1]

---

[1] For a fuller discussion of the authorship of *Henry VIII*, see my
British Academy Shakespeare lecture for 1931, *Shakespeare's Iterative
Imagery*, Oxford University Press, 1931, pp. 22, 23.

G. WILSON KNIGHT

A Note on Henry VIII

I

Perhaps no other Shakespearian play presents so queer a case of academic disintegration and uncritical popularity. Scholars have for long written off the most important scenes as the work of Fletcher, while asserting that the whole lacks unity and design. This position has hitherto been left unchallenged. Actors have, however, generally recognized the greatness at least of individual scenes and persons in the play. Irving played Wolsey with Forbes-Robertson as a famous Buckingham.[1] *Henry VIII* was one of Tree's most successful productions, and Wolsey one of his best parts. Since the war Dame Sybil Thorndike has played Queen Katharine, and Charles Laughton, more recently still, Henry himself. The play appeals to the profession. The general public have mainly followed the actor's rather than the professorial lead. They have not been unduly disquieted about "feminine" endings; and, I think, rightly. Here I wish to plot out a short interpreta-

From *Shakespeare and Religion* by G. Wilson Knight. New York: Barnes & Noble, Inc.; London: Routledge & Kegan Paul Ltd., 1967. Reprinted by permission of the publishers.
[1] There is a gramophone record easily obtainable of Forbes-Robertson's speaking of Buckingham's great speech, which Mr. Granville-Barker, in his lecture *From Henry V to Hamlet* (*Aspects of Shakespeare*, Oxford University Press) has called "the most beautiful piece of speaking I ever heard." I understand Mr. Granville-Barker's aspersion on "such creaking methods"; but I nevertheless suggest that anyone who thinks the speech is by Fletcher should buy the record and play it from time to time.

tion maturing from acceptance of the play's artistic and organic validity. Afterwards, I return to the question of authorship.

II

The King here is not the middle-aged, sensual, robustious, goodhearted but expeditious wife-killer whose successful promiscuity has endeared him to the hearts of the British public. He can be best placed by considering the response we make to such a stage-direction as: "Flourish: Enter King and Attendants." He is not primarily a character study and should certainly not be performed as a "character" part. Primarily he is King of England; dignified, still young, honorable, and every inch a King. We must not let our sympathy for Katharine and our knowledge of a certain self-deception within Henry's supposedly conscience-stricken desire to divorce her—both have undoubted support in the play—prevent our recognition of his central position and sacred office. For this is recognized, and stressed, by all the persons. The others do not blame him; nor should we. Certainly, during the early acts he is a little insecure, deceiving himself once, deceived by others often, and distraught by troublesome rivalries and ambitions. But at the end he is a king of power and a peace-maker, overruling all turbulent and envious discontents. Which brings us to another important thought.

The play is epic rather than dramatic in structure; or, perhaps, an epic which includes a succession of single dramatic movements. Three of these show an important similarity. Buckingham opposes Wolsey's ambitious scheming and quickly falls under an apparently false charge of treason. He was formerly haughty, aristocratic, intolerant. But he goes to his death already "half in heaven," forgiving all his enemies, praying for the King, a martyr of Christ-like strength. A sudden reversal, but more than paralleled by the fall of Wolsey. Wolsey is a crafty, unprincipled, and ambitious schemer and statesman. His indirect methods are exposed, the King's displeasure falls on him, and he next embraces a religious humility and poverty with only his robe and his "integrity to heaven" in place of his former glories. He preaches what is almost a sermon at his fall, urging Cromwell to serve the King without ambition, thus forgiving and honoring to the last the master who he nevertheless feels has been unjust and ungrateful to himself. He dies, as Griffeth tells us, in religious peace. Third, we have the tragedy of Katharine. She is shown first as a strong, almost domineering woman who hampers Wolsey's policy. At her trial she excels in innocent and wronged dignity, and shows scathing scorn of what she considers Wolsey's injustice and hypocrisy, a theme developed further in her subsequent scene with the two Cardinals. But her story closes too in religious light. She hears of Wolsey's death, prays for his rest, showing, however, that she is not yet free from bitterness towards him; next listens to Griffeth's noble eulogy—which is, perhaps, necessary to stimulate our forgiveness too—and at last attains to perfect charity towards her wronger. Whereupon follows her Vision, in which angelic figures, to solemn music, offer her the garland of immortality from the land of that "celestial harmony" that awaits her. She dies blessing the King, like the rest, without resentment.

Notice how with all these we are never quite clear as to faults and virtues, the exact rights and wrongs of it all, but the rhythm from personal pride and sense of injustice and unkindness—each endures the typical Shakespearian sense of betrayal by friend or lover—to Christian humility, absolute forgiveness, and religious peace is found in each. It must be observed, too, how service to the King is uppermost in the thoughts of all at their end and is inextricably twined with the thought of duty toward God. Thus is unrolled the sequence of individual tragic movements. The play is rich with both a grand royalism and a thrilling but solemn Christianity; orthodox religious coloring being present and powerful throughout far in excess of any previous play.

But there is more, of less tragic impact. Countering and interwoven with these we have the rise of Anne Bullen. The King meets her in a scene of revelry and dance, and she has a gorgeous coronation, staged for us by direction and description. She is presented as a lovable and beautiful woman, and we are pointed by choric passages to rejoice in the King's good fortune. The play culminates in the christening of her child and the striking prophecy of Cranmer. These happier elements are mostly associated with the future Protestantism of England—hence the importance of Cranmer—whereas the tragic elements are entwined rather with the Cardinals, the Pope, and Roman Catholicism generally. The movement from Queen Katharine to Anne Bullen is thus, partly at least, a religious movement. Nor can the play be properly understood without a clear sight of its amazing conclusion, to which the whole surge of the epic advances. Cranmer's prophecy is the justification and explanation of all that precedes it.

All these themes radiate from the central figure of the King. He is like a rock, the others are waves breaking round him. And he grows in dignity and power. Towards the end he dismisses the third trial in our story, that of Cranmer, enforcing peace and goodwill, and silencing the fiery Gardiner: all which is, of course, to be contrasted with the earlier unhappy trials of Buckingham and Katharine. So we have a most involved story-pattern in terms of a few years of one King's reign which nevertheless suggests a vast history and universal movement: the rise and fall of noble men and women, whose individual sufferings and deaths are in some way necessary to the structure of a greater than themselves, here the religious independence and national glory of England; and whose troubled stories, and the King's too, including his lapse from strict honesty with himself, are shown as necessary, or at all events preliminary, to their final flowering, justification and perfection in the child Elizabeth. Thus in producing the play it is perhaps best to mark it into three act-divisions: two mainly tragic, the third optimistic. The first ends with the execution of Buckingham and the second with the fall of Wolsey; the third presenting a rising action with the coronation of Anne Bullen, Katharine's Vision—which may be allowed to suggest the peace in eternity that has also received Buckingham and Wolsey—Cranmer's trial and reinstatement, the final christening, and the prophetic conclusion forecasting the happy reigns of Elizabeth and James I.

So the mystic riches of that eternity which bounds human tragedy here alternate with the more temporal glories of successful kingship, and both contribute to the inspired words of Cranmer over the new-christened Elizabeth, foretelling a divinely ordered prosperity, worship, and peace. That such blending of national and religious prophecy should be centered on a child is nothing strange: Isaiah and Virgil offer interesting correspondences.[2] And, indeed, the final scene of *Henry VIII* is in essence close to a medieval, or modern, nativity play: and as such should it be rendered in the theater.

III

I shall now briefly notice *Henry VIII* in relation to Shakespeare's other work. I need not recapitulate in any detail what I have elsewhere written on Shakespeare's final plays. But it may be as well to repeat that they are saturated in religious transcendentalism and present plots mainly concerned with loss in tempest, jealousy, misfortune, and all evils, balanced against divine appearances, and the resurrection of lost loves to music, with a general stress on oracles, dreams, prophecies and chapels. These plays, following the somber plays, seem to represent a certain inward progress of the poet's informing genius from tragedy to religious light. They and the tragedies may all be called "personal" in comparison with the earlier histories. *The Tempest* presents a final and comprehensive synthesis of the poet's main intuitions, Prospero's farewell to his art thus resembling, inevitably and with no necessary trick of conscious allegory, something of what Shakespeare the man might be supposed to feel on looking back over his completed work. Prospero

2 See T. F. Royds, *Vergil & Isaiah* (Blackwell): an admirable short study of that very entwining of spiritual prophecy with national affairs which I find in *Henry VIII*. This book has helped my general understanding.

leaves his island to embrace again the community of men; and Shakespeare the artist writes another play with a theme national rather than personal and philosophic, an impregnating mythology Christian rather than pseudo-Hellenic or elsewise pagan, and a prophetic finale referring primarily to the two sovereigns under whose reign he has lived.

It is a logical conclusion enough. There is something almost inevitable about this play coming at this time. It is crammed, too, with reminders of the other final plays. Queen Katharine on trial before her own husband is almost a reincarnation of Hermione; as later, listening to music to solace her marital distress, she reminds us of Desdemona. Her Vision repeats, in Christian terms, the theophanies to which the others have accustomed us—the oracle of Delphi and the appearance of Apollo described in *The Winter's Tale,* Diana in *Pericles,* Jupiter in *Cymbeline;* and, of course, much of the same sort in *The Tempest.* In close connection with each of these—except only the examples from *The Tempest*—occurs the rare word "celestial," used too by Katharine just before her visionary sleep. The recurrent forgiveness-motif in *Henry VIII* presents exactly the quality and depth of Prospero's forgiveness. Most important of all, the birth and child themes of the other final plays are reflected here in the glorification of the baptized child Elizabeth. I have elsewhere claimed that the restoration of Hermione and Thaisa to their husbands may be said to correspond to an intuition of a paradisal eternity such as that which lies behind, or may be said to lie behind, the restoration of Beatrice to Dante or Gretchen to Faust; whereas the finding of the lost child, Perdita or Marina, and, I might add, the importance given to the various children's happiness and success at the last moments of all the final plays, suggests rather the onward progress of creation within time; the words "time" and "eternity" being here deliberately used as metaphysical concepts arbitrarily applied to a poetic creation to bridge the gap between art and thought. Now in *Henry VIII* we find a similar contrast. Queen Katharine's vision of eternal bliss is set di-

rectly beside the more humanly joyous coronation of
Anne Bullen, and not long after we have the baptismal
ceremony of the infant Elizabeth. Notice how much happier this contrast is than the more cruel juxtaposition
earlier of the King's revelling in Wolsey's Palace immediately before Buckingham's execution. It is as though
time and eternity were seen converging as the play un-
furls, to meet in exquisite union at Cranmer's prophecy:
which again may remind us of the soothsayer and the
prophetic conclusion of *Cymbeline*.

If in *The Tempest* Shakespeare gives us a comprehensive and inclusive statement of his furthest spiritual
adventures, in *Henry VIII* he has gone yet further, directly relating those adventures to the religion of his day
and the nation of his birth. In the prophecy of Cranmer
I see the culmination not only of the epic movement of
Henry VIII as a whole but the point where the vast
tributary of Shakespeare's work from *Hamlet* to *The
Tempest* enters the wider waters of a nation's historic and
religious advance, to swell "the main of floods" to England's glory and, through her, the establishment of the
peace of Christ on earth.

IV

All this, I shall be told, would be well enough, if there
were ten syllables in each line of the great speeches here
and not eleven. Frankly, I do not know how satisfactorily
to answer this objection: because I do not understand it.
I believe such pseudo-scientific theorizing is again here,
as elsewhere, merely an unconscious projection of our
sense of organic incoherence within the play due to failure in focus and understanding. *Henry VIII* is generally
divided into scenes of what is usually considered "ordi-
nary" Shakespearian verse, and those where there is a
high percentage of eleven-syllable lines. Now, if these
latter are by Fletcher,[3] we certainly have not an instance

3 The late Edgar I. Fripp once strongly opposed the Fletcherian theory
in a letter written to me about my first Shakespearian publication *Myth
and Miracle*, suggesting, if I remember right, that I should incorporate
Henry VIII in my general thesis. His letter redirected my attention to a
play I had not then read for some years.

of Fletcher spoiling the Shakespearian art-form by weak collaboration, but rather, if we cannot, because of variation in style, see the play as an organic whole, we must observe Shakespeare trying (in vain) to spoil a Fletcherian masterpiece—since it is the best scenes that are considered un-Shakespearian; a masterpiece in some ways —in a certain selfless and Christian nobility and finality of restrained power—greater than anything Shakespeare had done himself outside *The Tempest*. But there is surely no necessity for all this. Shakespeare had long —in the latter acts of *Timon* for example—been finding the extra syllable a means, when he wanted it, to verbal mastery of an especially grand but reserved strength of statement. In *The Tempest* it is continual: Act V alone provides all the examples any one should want. In *Henry VIII* this style is finely used to mark the solemn cadences of the grandest scenes: Buckingham's Farewell, Katharine's Trial, her interview with Wolsey and Campeius, Wolsey's Fall, Katharine's Vision, Cranmer's Prophecy. And I find, on reinspection, that the admittedly Shakespearian scenes have a goodly sprinkling of it too. Indeed, Shakespeare has only here carried a certain technical effect, which he had for some time been progressively and increasingly developing and had brought to a climax in *The Tempest,* just a little further than before, emphasizing it especially in the most important scenes according to the quality of the occasion.

Moreover, these noble speeches are rich in the cadences of typical Shakespearian emotion and Shakespearian thought; though the expression is restrained, as in *The Tempest,* the metaphors are likewise Shakespearian;[4] and the general power is, indeed, such that, if Fletcher wrote

---

4 Miss Spurgeon certainly notes that a single typical strand of Shakespearian imagery is not found in the suspected scenes, while it is found elsewhere. But imagery and rhythm both naturally vary with scenic tone. And it is pleasant to find Miss Spurgeon writing that the evidence of imagery "by no means all points one way," and expressing her belief that Shakespeare "wrote the greater part of the play." (*Shakespeare's Iterative Imagery* in *Aspects of Shakespeare,* Oxford University Press.)

them, he was clearly one of the two greatest poets in our literature, sharing that honor alone with the author of *Timon* and *The Tempest,* to whom he bears so striking and uncanny a resemblance.

227

MARK VAN DOREN

Henry VIII

Shakespeare's rest could not have been interrupted long by *Henry VIII,* even if he wrote every word of it. It has become a tradition to say that only five or six scenes are his, and that Fletcher, or possibly Massinger, is responsible for the remainder; although one extreme theory gives him the entire work, and another takes it all away. The question has interest, not because *Henry VIII* is important in itself but because in any view it is an imitation of Shakespeare; it is at the same time like him and unlike him. And the question will not be answered because in such cases we cannot know whether the poet has imitated himself or been imitated by another.

A certain resemblance to Shakespeare's later plays is all too obvious. Tempests, shores, flowers, music, and peace are incidental themes. Henry knows how to praise Katherine in the idiom of Pericles and Florizel: she is "the queen of earthly queens" (II.iv.141), and her saint-like meekness is most rare. And reconciliation is rampant —several dramas, rather than one, busily develop it into a kind of orthodoxy.

Just there the resemblance ceases; or overleaps its limits and lands in imitation. For the successive dramas in which Buckingham, Katherine, Wolsey, and Cranmer

From *Shakespeare* by Mark Van Doren. Copyright 1939, © 1967 by Mark Van Doren. Reprinted by permission of Holt, Rinehart and Winston, Inc.

submit their wills to Henry's are not dramas of reconciliation. The theme has been watered down; resignation is now the word, and its repetition through a series of unmotivated surrenders suggests machinery. Either Shakespeare has lost the impulse which gave his final stories their mellow power, or some other poet has never felt it. Three proud persons break suddenly and bow before a dummy king who represents England, and a fourth who has never been "unsound," Archbishop Cranmer, basks weeping in the sun of his accepted monarch. It is like nine-pins going down, nor can we miss a tone of smugness in the proud ones as they pray. This is Buckingham:

> Go with me, like good angels, to my end;
> And, as the long divorce of steel falls on me,
> Make of your prayers one sweet sacrifice,
> And lift my soul to heaven.   (II.i.75–8)

This is Katherine:

> Remember me
> In all humility unto his Highness.
> Say his long trouble now is passing
> Out of this world; tell him, in death I bless'd him,
> For so I will.   (IV.ii.160–4)

And this is Wolsey:

> Nay then, farewell!
> I have touch'd the highest point of all my greatness;
> And, from that full meridian of my glory,
> I haste now to my setting. I shall fall
> Like a bright exhalation in the evening,
> And no man see me more. . . .
> I have ventur'd,
> Like little wanton boys that swim on bladders,
> This many summers in a sea of glory,
> But far beyond my depth. My high-blown pride
> At length broke under me, and now has left me,
> Weary and old with service, to the mercy
> Of a rude stream, that must for ever hide me. . . .

O Cromwell, Cromwell!
Had I but serv'd my God with half the zeal
I serv'd my king, He would not in mine age
Have left me naked to mine enemies.   (III.ii.222–457)

The smugness of their tone goes with a smoothness in their verse such as Shakespeare had long ago outgrown. Not for years had he let his lines roll like this, or ripened his metaphors to rottenness. "Highest point," "meridian," "setting," "bright exhalation in the evening"—there is too much of it by Shakespeare's final standard, and although it is excellent in its way it bears no resemblance to the unique elliptical poetry he had recently been writing. "Swim on bladders," "sea of glory," "high-blown pride," "rude stream"—any competent poet could have developed the image thus, just as any workman of 1612 or 1613 could have worked out the vegetable autobiography of Wolsey in terms of his tender leaves, his blossoms, his blushing honors, his greatness ripening, and his root nipped on the third day by a killing frost (III.ii. 352–8).

The style of any good poet moves from simplicity to congestion, and once this end is reached return is difficult if not impossible. If Shakespeare returned in *Henry VIII* he was performing an extraordinary feat. He had performed many feats in his history, but not this one, of which nevertheless he was perhaps capable. At the same time, however, and in the same play, he imitated—or someone did—his last nervous style. It crops out everywhere, not only in the scenes assigned to him but in some that are assigned to his collaborator.

The tract of everything
Would by a good discourser lose some life,
Which action's self was tongue to.   (I.i.40–2)

Of her that loves him with that excellence
That angels love good men with.   (II.ii.34–5)

And which gifts,
Saving your mincing, the capacity

Of your soft cheveril conscience would receive,
If you might please to stretch it.   (II.iii.30–3)

For it is you
Have blown this coal betwixt my lord and me,
Which God's dew quench!   (II.iv.78–80)

If your business
Seek me out, and that way I am wife in,
Out with it boldly.   (III.i.37–9)

Such a noise arose
As the shrouds make at sea in a stiff tempest,
As loud, and to as many tunes. . . . No man living
Could say "This is my wife" there; all were woven
So strangely in one piece.   (IV.i.71–81)

These are imitations in the sense that their virtue has no
bulk, their involutions no excuse. They may or may not
have been written by Shakespeare, but it does not matter.
They do not save the play for distinction any more than
its gorgeous pageants make up for an absence of drama,
or than its external compliments to Oxford and Cambridge, Elizabeth and James, have continued after three
centuries to be interesting. The two styles in *Henry VIII*
are two currents of water, one tepid and the other icy.
The difference is to be noted, but it is also to be noted
that the water is never wine.

The style of certain passages in *The Two Noble Kinsmen* which criticism persists in suspecting to be Shakespeare's gives us a headier imitation of his brew.

Draw thy fear'd sword
That does good turns to th' world.   (I.i.48–9)

O queen Emilia,
Fresher than May, sweeter
Than her gold buttons on the boughs or all
Th' enamell'd knacks o' the mead or garden! Yea,
We challenge too the bank of any nymph,
That makes the stream seem flowers! Thou, O jewel

O' th' wood, o' th' world, hast likewise bless'd a place
With thy sole presence.   (III.i.4–11)

          Each stroke laments
The place whereon it falls, and sounds more like
A bell than blade.   (V.iii.4–6)

But it is imitation, and once again the identity of its
contriver does not matter. The lines are charming in their
oddity rather than beautiful in their strength; the syntax
is wrenched, the syllables are curled, for no discoverable
reason. The quaint series of little triumphs grows tire-
somely long, together with a story which cannot be
believed and whose two fine heroes talk like one gold-
plated man. The shortness of breath in Shakespeare's later
verse was a sign of seriousness and power; here after a
while it is weakness, for this verse lives only within the
phrase, dying at each fall to gasp again. Such cleverness
is senseless, as Shakespeare in his right mind never was.
It drones, as he never did. None of his styles was an end
in itself as this one is. He wrote to further ends: to say
things, to tell stories, to mingle lives with lives. His one
great end he could never have wished to put into a few
words. Nor did he need to, since his many words would
last.

Suggested References

The number of possible references is vast and grows alarmingly. (The *Shakespeare Quarterly* devotes a substantial part of one issue each year to a list of the previous year's work, and *Shakespeare Survey*—an annual publication—includes a substantial review of recent scholarship, as well as an occasional essay surveying a few decades of scholarship on a chosen topic.) Though no works are indispensable, those listed below have been found helpful.

1. Shakespeare's Times

Byrne, M. St. Clare. *Elizabethan Life in Town and Country*. Rev. ed. New York: Barnes & Noble, Inc., 1961. Chapters on manners, beliefs, education, etc., with illustrations.

Craig, Hardin. *The Enchanted Glass: the Elizabethan Mind in Literature*. New York and London: Oxford University Press, 1936. The Elizabethan intellectual climate.

Nicoll, Allardyce (ed.). *The Elizabethans*. London: Cambridge University Press, 1957. An anthology of Elizabethan writings, especially valuable for its illustrations from paintings, title pages, etc.

Shakespeare's England. 2 vols. Oxford: The Clarendon Press, 1916. A large collection of scholarly essays on a wide variety of topics (e.g., astrology, costume, gardening, horsemanship), with special attention to Shakespeare's references to these topics.

Tillyard, E. M. W. *The Elizabethan World Picture*. London: Chatto & Windus, 1943; New York: The Macmillan Company, 1944. A brief account of some Elizabethan ideas of the universe.

Wilson, John Dover (ed.). *Life in Shakespeare's England.* 2nd ed. New York: The Macmillan Company, 1913. An anthology of Elizabethan writings on the countryside, superstition, education, the court, etc.

2. Shakespeare

Bentley, Gerald Eades. *Shakespeare: A Biographical Handbook.* New Haven, Conn.: Yale University Press, 1961. The facts about Shakespeare, with virtually no conjecture intermingled.

Bradby, Anne (ed.). *Shakespeare Criticism, 1919–1935.* London: Oxford University Press, 1936. A small anthology of excellent essays on the plays.

Bush, Geoffrey. *Shakespeare and the Natural Condition.* Cambridge, Mass.: Harvard University Press; London: Oxford University Press, 1956. A short sensitive account of Shakespeare's view of "Nature," touching most of the works.

Chambers, E. K. *William Shakespeare: A Study of Facts and Problems.* 2 vols. London: Oxford University Press, 1930. An invaluable, detailed reference work; not for the casual reader.

Chute, Marchette. *Shakespeare of London.* New York: E. P. Dutton & Co., Inc., 1949. A readable biography fused with portraits of Stratford and London life.

Clemen, Wolfgang H. *The Development of Shakespeare's Imagery.* Cambridge, Mass.: Harvard University Press, 1951. (Originally published in German, 1936.) A temperate account of a subject often abused.

Craig, Hardin. *An Interpretation of Shakespeare.* Columbia, Missouri: Lucas Brothers, 1948. A scholar's book designed for the layman. Comments on all the works.

Dean, Leonard F. (ed.). *Shakespeare: Modern Essays in Criticism.* New York: Oxford University Press, 1957. Mostly mid-twentieth-century critical studies, covering Shakespeare's artistry.

Granville-Barker, Harley. *Prefaces to Shakespeare.* 2 vols.

Princeton, N.J.: Princeton University Press, 1946–47. Essays on ten plays by a scholarly man of the theater.

Harbage, Alfred. *As They Liked It*. New York: The Macmillan Company, 1947. A sensitive, long essay on Shakespeare, morality, and the audience's expectations.

Ridler, Anne Bradby (ed.). *Shakespeare Criticism, 1935–1960*. New York and London: Oxford University Press, 1963. An excellent continuation of the anthology edited earlier by Miss Bradby (see above).

Smith, D. Nichol (ed.). *Shakespeare Criticism*. New York: Oxford University Press, 1916. A selection of criticism from 1623 to 1840, ranging from Ben Jonson to Thomas Carlyle.

Spencer, Theodore. *Shakespeare and the Nature of Man*. New York: The Macmillan Company, 1942. Shakespeare's plays in relation to Elizabethan thought.

Stoll, Elmer Edgar. *Shakespeare and Other Masters*. Cambridge, Mass.: Harvard University Press; London: Oxford University Press, 1940. Essays on tragedy, comedy, and aspects of dramaturgy, with special reference to some of Shakespeare's plays.

Traversi, D. A. *An Approach to Shakespeare*. Rev. ed. New York: Doubleday & Co., Inc., 1956. An analysis of the plays, beginning with words, images, and themes, rather than with characters.

Van Doren, Mark. *Shakespeare*. New York: Henry Holt & Company, Inc., 1939. Brief, perceptive readings of all of the plays.

Whitaker, Virgil K. *Shakespeare's Use of Learning*. San Marino, Calif.: Huntington Library, 1953. A study of the relation of Shakespeare's reading to his development as a dramatist.

3. Shakespeare's Theater

Adams, John Cranford. *The Globe Playhouse*. Rev. ed. New York: Barnes & Noble, Inc., 1961. A detailed conjecture about the physical characteristics of the theater Shakespeare often wrote for.

Beckerman, Bernard. *Shakespeare at the Globe, 1599–1609*. New York: The Macmillan Company, 1962. On the playhouse and on Elizabethan dramaturgy, acting, and staging.

Chambers, E. K. *The Elizabethan Stage*. 4 vols. New York: Oxford University Press, 1923. Reprinted with corrections, 1945. An invaluable reference work on theaters, theatrical companies, and staging at court.

Harbage, Alfred. *Shakespeare's Audience*. New York: Columbia University Press; London: Oxford University Press, 1941. A study of the size and nature of the theatrical public.

Hodges, C. Walter. *The Globe Restored*. London: Ernest Benn, Ltd., 1953; New York: Coward-McCann, Inc., 1954. A well-illustrated and readable attempt to reconstruct the Globe Theatre.

Kernodle, George R. *From Art to Theatre: Form and Convention in the Renaissance*. Chicago: University of Chicago Press, 1944. Pioneering and stimulating work on the symbolic and cultural meanings of theater construction.

Nagler, A. M. *Shakespeare's Stage*. Tr. by Ralph Manheim. New Haven, Conn.: Yale University Press, 1958. An excellent brief introduction to the physical aspect of the playhouse.

Smith, Irwin. *Shakespeare's Globe Playhouse*. New York: Charles Scribner's Sons, 1957. Chiefly indebted to J. C. Adams' controversial book, with additional material and scale drawings for model-builders.

Venezky, Alice S. *Pageantry on the Shakespearean Stage*. New York: Twayne Publishers, Inc., 1951. An examination of spectacle in Elizabethan drama.

4. Miscellaneous Reference Works

Abbott, E. A. *A Shakespearean Grammar*. New edition. New York: The Macmillan Company, 1877. An examination of differences between Elizabethan and modern grammar.

Bartlett, John. *A New and Complete Concordance . . . to . . . Shakespeare*. New York: The Macmillan Company, 1894. An index to most of Shakespeare's words.

Berman, Ronald. *A Reader's Guide to Shakespeare's*

Plays. Chicago: Scott, Foresman and Company, 1965. A short bibliography of the chief articles and books on each play.

Bullough, Geoffrey. *Narrative and Dramatic Sources of Shakespeare.* 6 vols. Vol. 7 in preparation. New York: Columbia University Press; London: Routledge & Kegan Paul, Ltd., 1957–. A collection of many of the books Shakespeare drew upon.

Greg, W. W. *The Shakespeare First Folio.* New York and London: Oxford University Press, 1955. A detailed yet readable history of the first collection (1623) of Shakespeare's plays.

Kökeritz, Helge. *Shakespeare's Names.* New Haven, Conn.: Yale University Press, 1959; London: Oxford University Press, 1960. A guide to the pronunciation of some 1,800 names appearing in Shakespeare.

———. *Shakespeare's Pronunciation.* New Haven, Conn.: Yale University Press; London: Oxford University Press, 1953. Contains much information about puns and rhymes.

Linthicum, Marie C. *Costume in the Drama of Shakespeare and His Contemporaries.* New York and London: Oxford University Press, 1936. On the fabrics and dress of the age, and references to them in the plays.

Muir, Kenneth. *Shakespeare's Sources.* London: Methuen & Co., Ltd., 1957. Vol. 2 in preparation. The first volume, on the comedies and tragedies, attempts to ascertain what books were Shakespeare's sources, and what use he made of them.

Onions, C. T. *A Shakespeare Glossary.* London: Oxford University Press, 1911; 2nd ed., rev., with enlarged addenda, 1953. Definitions of words (or senses of words) now obsolete.

Partridge, Eric. *Shakespeare's Bawdy.* Rev. ed. New York: E. P. Dutton & Co., Inc.; London: Routledge & Kegan Paul, Ltd., 1955. A glossary of bawdy words and phrases.

Shakespeare Quarterly. See headnote to Suggested References.

Shakespeare Survey. See headnote to Suggested References.

Smith, Gordon Ross. *A Classified Shakespeare Bibliography 1936–1958*. University Park, Pa.: Pennsylvania State University Press, 1963. A list of some 20,000 items on Shakespeare.

5. *Henry VIII*

Alexander, Peter. "Conjectural History, or Shakespeare's *Henry VIII*," *Essays and Studies,* XVI (1930), 85–120.

Bertram, Paul. *Shakespeare and "The Two Noble Kinsmen."* New Brunswick, New Jersey: Rutgers University Press, 1965. [Contains a chapter on *"Henry VIII:* The Consequences of a Problem of Authorship."]

Byrne, Muriel St. Clare. "A Stratford Production: *Henry VIII,*" *Shakespeare Survey 3* (1950), 120–29. [A review of the 1949 Guthrie performance.]

Felperin, Howard. "Shakespeare's *Henry VIII:* History as Myth," *Studies in English Literature: 1500–1900,* VI (1966), 225–46.

Foakes, R. A. (ed.). *The Arden Edition of the Works of William Shakespeare: King Henry VIII.* London: Methuen & Co., Ltd., 1957.

Kermode, Frank. "What Is Shakespeare's *Henry VIII* About?", *Durham University Journal,* N.S., IX (1947–48), 48–55.

Knight, G. Wilson. *The Crown of Life: Essays in Interpretation of Shakespeare's Final Plays.* New York and London: Oxford University Press, 1947; New York: Barnes & Noble, Inc., 1966 (University Paperbacks).

Leech, Clifford. "The Structure of the Last Plays," *Shakespeare Survey 11* (1958), 19–30.

Maxwell, J. C. (ed.). *The New Shakespeare: King Henry the Eighth.* Cambridge, England: Cambridge University Press, 1962.

Mincoff, Marco. *"Henry VIII* and Fletcher," *Shakespeare Quarterly,* XII (1961), 239–60.

Reese, Max Meredith. *The Cease of Majesty: A Study of Shakespeare's History Plays.* New York: St. Martin's

Press, Inc., 1962; London: Edward Arnold (Publishers) Ltd., 1961.

Ribner, Irving. *The English History Play in the Age of Shakespeare*. 2nd ed., revised. London: Methuen & Co., Ltd., 1965.

Wasson, John. "In Defense of *King Henry VIII*," *Research Studies* (1964), 261–76 (Washington State University).

The SIGNET Classic Shakespeare

Already available at 50¢ each